WITHDRAWN

AMERICAN WOMEN IN

SPORT, 1887-1987

a 100-year chronology

compiled by

Ruth M. Sparhawk

Mary E. Leslie

Phyllis Y. Turbow

Zina R. Rose

THE SCARECROW PRESS, INC.
Metuchen, N.J., & London
1989

British Library Cataloguing-in-Publication data available

Library of Congress Cataloging-in-Publication Data

American women in sport, 1887-1987.

   Bibliography: p.
   Includes indexes.
   1. Women athletes--United States--History--Chronology.
2. Sports for women--United States--History--Chronology.
I. Sparhawk, Ruth M., 1923-
CV583.A64 1989   796'.0194   89-6150
ISBN 0-8108-2205-9

Copyright © 1989 by Ruth M. Sparhawk, Mary E. Leslie,
   Phyllis Y. Turbow, and Zina R. Rose
Manufactured in the United States of America

This work is dedicated
to the women athletes of America--
past, present, and future

CONTENTS

ACKNOWLEDGMENTS

There is a definite need for a chronology of women in sport. As a teacher of sport history at the University of Southern California, I have been bothered by not having a ready reference to those individuals who have made immeasurable contributions to the growth and development of women in sport.

In the late 1970s, I started the compilation of a chronology. Time constraints did not allow me to complete the research on my own. Zina Rose and Mary Leslie accepted the challenge and joined the project. To enhance the team effort, Phyllis Turbow also became involved. Each member of the team has made a positive contribution to this endeavor. The project could not have been completed without their talent. I wish to give each one credit and praise for her energy, expertise, and loyalty.

Many other people helped in the completion of this chronology:

Mary V. Ebersole and Hugh and Mary Leslie continued to clip relevant articles, from well before the endeavor was begun to well after it was finished.

Betty Hennessy and Holly Curtis read critically and helped to weed out inconsistencies in the initial drafts.

Blake Wilson had the most difficult task of all-- locating information. His hours of research and organization enabled us to update and complete a chronology of achievements that changed daily.

In the final stages of production, the manuscript was prepared, proofread, and checked by the very reliable Patsy

Sullivan, Donna Finch, Waunda Strickland, Jack Riley, and
Ruth and Leo Young.

Many organizations contributed information and photo-
graphs for inclusion in this book. The names of these groups
are listed at the back of this volume.

Ruth M. Sparhawk
Professor Emerita
University of
Southern
California

PREFACE

Women have been participating in sports for thousands of years. There is evidence that the women of ancient Egypt played games. The young girls in ancient Greece had their own Olympic Games, as they were not allowed to participate in or watch the men's Games. Long before the first colonists came to this country, Native American women engaged in sports activities. Eighteenth- and nineteenth-century American women paved the way for the athletes of today.

The women's movement, the enactment of Title IX by the U.S. Congress, and the provision of increased media coverage for women's athletics have all helped to focus public attention on women in sports. The purpose of this book is to recognize the accomplishments of American women athletes in the 100 years from 1887 to 1987.

We have divided this era into four time periods based on the societal views of women in sport as well as on the changing organizational control of women's athletic competition in the United States. Each of the four periods will be treated as a separate chapter.

In each chapter, we have designed a year-by-year chronology of significant events in the world of women's sports. By definition, a chronology is merely a list. We have elected to recognize as many individuals as possible and to let their accomplishments speak for themselves. Although there is undoubtedly a fascinating story behind each athlete and her achievements, the limitations of time and space prevented us from providing all of the details.

In every historical endeavor, a degree of bias is present. We acknowledge that we may indeed have omitted notable individuals and accomplishments from this work, but we

assure the reader that any omissions are purely unintentional.
We believe that we have presented as comprehensive a listing
as possible.

While reading this chronology, try to observe the
types of sports that are listed most frequently in the various
time periods--for instance more individual sports in the
early years and more team sports in the contemporary eras.
It may be possible to get a feeling for the changing attitudes
of society and of the athletes themselves.

It is our hope that this will be a useful reference
book, but more important, a much-needed addition to the
existing women's sports literature. Read it all at once,
or by chapters, or by individual years--or follow your fa-
vorite athlete throughout her career. We trust that you
will encounter some familiar names. We also expect that
you will meet several athletes whose names are not well known,
but whose accomplishments are obviously deserving of recognition.

ABBREVIATIONS

AAAPE--American Association for the Advancement of Physical Education

AAHPER--American Alliance for Health, Physical Education, and Recreation

AAU--Amateur Athletic Union

ABC--American Bowling Congress

ACACW--Athletic Conference of American College Women

AIAW--Association for Intercollegiate Athletics for Women

ASA--Amateur Softball Association

ATA--Amateur Trapshooting Association

BPAA--Bowling Proprietors' Association of America

BWAA--Bowling Writers Association of America

CIAW--Commission on Intercollegiate Athletics for Women

CWA--Committee on Women's Athletics

DGWS--Division for Girls' and Women's Sports

FIQ--International Federation of Bowlers [Fédération Internationale des Quillieurs]

GAH--Grand American Handicap

IOC--International Olympic Committee

IWBA--International Women's Bowling Association

LPGA--Ladies Professional Golf Association

NAA--National Archery Association

NAGWS--National Association for Girls and Women in Sport

NAIA--National Association of Intercollegiate Athletics

NCAA--National Collegiate Athletic Association

NFR--National Finals Rodeo

NJCAA--National Junior College Athletic Association

NRA--National Rifle Association

PAA--Professional Archers Association

PBAA--Professional Bowlers Association of America

PWBA--Professional Women Bowlers Association

SCAA--Southern California Athletic Association

TAC--The Athletics Congress

USLTA--United States Lawn Tennis Association

USOC--United States Olympic Committee

USTFF--United States Track and Field Finals

USVBA--United States Volleyball Association

WBA--Women's Bowling Association

WIBC--Women's International Bowling Congress

INTRODUCTION

Dame Julia, the first English woman to be recognized in print, was also the first to enter the exclusively male domain of sport in modern times. She was a Catholic nun and an avid angler, and she wrote authoritatively on various angling techniques, poles, hooks, and baits. Her publication of the Treatyse of Fishing with an Angle in 1492 preceded Izaak Walton's Compleat Angler by two hundred years.

Margot of Hainult, a fifteenth-century woman of France, was recognized as an expert in "royal" or "court" tennis, which was played simply with the bare hand. It was said that Margot could hit a backhand or forehand as well as any man in her day.

Mary, Queen of Scots, played golf in the sixteenth century. Her attendants were her young military aides-- her caddies. In the eighteenth century, Mary Wollstonecraft Shelley wrote about the need for physical education in the schooling of young women.

In 1811, the first known women's golf tournament was held at Musselburgh Golf Club in Scotland. The contestants were the town fishwives.

But these were isolated--and rare--examples of women's participation in physical activities. Victorian ideals governed the social conduct of women in the nineteenth century. Women were expected to maintain a delicate image. Accepted patterns of behavior for women reflected frailty, ill health, and weakness.

Catharine Beecher, a sister of Harriet Beecher Stowe, was one educator who attempted to change the attitudes of

society. In 1824, she organized the Female Seminary in
Hartford, Connecticut, and in 1837, she founded the Western
Female Institute in Cincinnati, Ohio (Gerber 1971). She de-
voted her talent and energy to the education of young women,
and she was among the first educators to emphasize the
value of formal programs of exercise and physical activity
for women. Between 1832 and 1870, she published several
books for the promotion of her ideas, which included Trea-
tise on Domestic Economy, Course of Calisthenics, and A
Manual of Physiology and Calisthenics for Schools and Fami-
lies. Her textbooks contained such thorough descriptions of
the proper methods of doing calisthenics that her programs
could be learned without an instructor. She suggested performing the exercises to musical accompaniment. Her goal
was to promote the development of a well-balanced mind and
a healthy body through the achievement of grace and good
posture.

Before 1887, the participation of women in sports was
restricted to noncompetitive recreational activities, including
bowling, croquet, golf, and horseback riding. Athletic
clubs provided opportunities for women to participate in
crew and fencing. Examples of American women's participation in sport during this period included skill exhibitions
in boxing, weight lifting, marksmanship, and ballooning.
A few women participated in "female pedestrianism" (long-
distance walking) or endurance swimming. In 1879, the
National Archery Association sponsored a public exhibition
of skill in which 20 women and 59 men took part.

Mary Ewing Outerbridge had a significant impact on
the development of sports for American women. Fascinated
by the game of tennis she had seen in England, she brought
the design for a lawn tennis court to the United States in
1874. She introduced the sport to American women, and by
1879, at least one woman had won a tennis championship.

During this period, the objective of sport participation
for women was not the development of physical vigor, but
the encouragement of respectable social encounters. Much
sport activity was restricted to members of the upper classes.
Women were accepted as spectators at horse races and ice
skating contests. In 1883, the first Ladies' Day baseball
game, where both "escorted" and "unescorted" women were
admitted free, was offered by the New York Giants.

The real breakthrough for American women in sport,
however, occurred at the Philadelphia Centennial in 1876.
It was there that the bicycle was introduced to the American
people. Suddenly, women literally had a vehicle for participation in physical activity. Shortly thereafter, Amelia Bloomer
designed nonrestrictive clothing ("bloomers") for women bi-
cyclists. More and more women wore these bloomers while
performing a variety of athletic activities, and a new era of
women's participation in sport was underway.

The modern history of American women's participation
in athletic competition can be divided into four periods:
the Pre-Organizational Era (1887-1916), the Organizational
Years (1917-1956), the Competitive Period (1957-1971), and
the Title IX Era (1972-1987) (Leslie 1979).

The Pre-Organizational Era was characterized by the
general disapproval of most types of athletic competition
for women. In American colleges, the control of women's
athletics was exerted almost entirely at the institutional
level by members of women's physical education faculties.

Several regulatory groups were founded during the
Organizational Years, including the Committee on Women's
Athletics, the Athletic Conference of American College Women,
and the Women's Division of the National Amateur Athletic
Federation. All of these organizations expressed their op-
position to the participation of American women in the 1932
Olympic Games.

The Competitive Period, which might more aptly be
termed the "Milk-and-Cookies Era," began in 1957. At this
time, the Division for Girls and Women's Sports (the updated
version of the Committee on Women's Athletics) acknowledged
the existence of intercollegiate athletic programs for women
in the United States. Athletic contests at schools and colleges were strictly regulated, but one constant feature of
competitive activity was postgame refreshments. Enjoying
milk and cookies with opposing players seemed to be a sure-
fire means of guaranteeing the social and recreational bene-
fits of physical activity. Despite the downplaying of competitive attitudes, women's athletics experienced significant
growth during this period.

In the 1960s, increased media coverage of women's

athletics was partially responsible for the development of
more favorable attitudes about women's participation in sports.
The enactment of Title IX of the Education Amendments of
1972 by the United States Congress helped to produce rapid
growth in the provision of competitive activities for women.

   Sport is no longer an exclusively male realm.   Today,
it is the domain of both females and males.   The phenomenal
growth in participation of girls and women in the last several
decades is due in large part to those girls and women who
said, "I can play, too."

   Welcome to the ever-changing world of women in sport!

I. THE PRE-ORGANIZATIONAL ERA
1887–1916

1887 Annie Oakley breaks her first 100 straight at trap-shooting in a match in London, setting a club record.

Rose Coghlan, in her initial attempt at trapshooting, breaks the ladies' amateur record and ties that of her amazed male competitors.

Eleven women compete in the United States Lawn Tennis Association matches.

1889 The United States Lawn Tennis Association extends its protective wing to "lady lawn tennis players."

1890 On January 25, Nellie Bly returns to New York from an unescorted trip around the world. Her modes of travel include ship, train, jinrikisha, and burro. Her record-setting 72-day, 6-hour, 11-minute journey raises some eyebrows, as it is unheard of for women-- even reporters--to travel in this manner.

1894 The faculty of Vassar College refuses a tennis challenge made to its students from the students of Bryn Mawr College.

1895 Mrs. C. S. Brown wins the first United States Golf Association's Women's Amateur Tournament.

At the age of 45, Annie Peck Smith scales Switzerland's famous Matterhorn.

1896   Thirteen women participate in the United States Cham-
        pion Golf Tournament sponsored by the United States
        Golf Association.

        The first intercollegiate basketball competitions for
        American women match the University of California-
        Berkeley against Leland Stanford University, and
        the University of Washington against Ellensburg Nor-
        mal School.

        Frankie Nelson covers 418 miles to win the first bicycle
        marathon for women.

        On the subject of women's competition in the Olympics,
        Pierre de Coubertin, reviver of the modern games, is
        quoted as saying, "We must continue to try to achieve
        the following definition: the solemn and periodic exal-
        tation of male athleticism with internationalism as a
        base, loyalty as a means, art for its setting, and fe-
        male applause as its reward" (quoted in Davenport
        1978, 58).

1899   Senda Berenson develops a set of basketball rules
        for women and introduces the game to her under-
        graduate students at Smith College.

        The American Association for the Advancement of Phys-
        ical Education (AAAPE) appoints a committee to study
        the various interpretations of women's basketball rules.
        The members include Senda Berenson, Alice Bertha
        Foster (Oberlin College), Ethel Perrin (Boston Normal
        School of Gymnastics), and Elizabeth Wright (Radcliffe
        College).

        Genevra Mudge, the first American woman to drive a
        race car, knocks down 5 spectators and then stalls
        her Locomobile in the snow while racing in New York
        City.

1900   Several Americans are among the first female contest-
        ants to participate in the modern Olympic Games.

        At the IInd Olympiad in Paris, Marion Jones Farquhar
        wins the bronze medal in tennis singles competition.

Margaret Abbot wins the gold medal in golf.

1901   The rules committee appointed by the AAAPE publishes
        the first basketball guide for women.

        Annie Taylor, a 43-year-old widow, survives her ride
        over Niagara Falls in a barrel.

1904   Although no women are permitted to compete in the
        IIIrd Olympiad in St. Louis as "official" contestants,
        several women enter the "unofficial" archery competi-
        tion, where an American woman--Lidia Howell--wins
        the gold medal. Mrs. Howell is the most successful
        woman archer in national competition. She will win
        the U.S. title 17 times in her career.

        Andrea Pollock wins the silver medal in archery, and
        Emma Cooke takes the bronze.

        Pinky Topperwein breaks 100 straight at trapshooting,
        a feat that she will accomplish over 200 times in her
        career.

        May Sutton of California wins the tennis championship
        of the United States.

        The Midwest Conference of Deans of Women registers
        its disapproval of women's intercollegiate athletic com-
        petition in the United States.

1905   May Sutton becomes the first American to win at Wimble-
        don, taking the women's singles title.

        Senda Berenson is appointed chairperson of the basket-
        ball rules committee of the AAAPE. The committee is
        the forerunner of the National Association for Girls and
        Women in Sport (NAGWS).

1906   Ellen Kelly organizes the first women's bowling league.

        Birdie Humphreys is a medal winner in special events held
        on the American Bowling Congress (ABC) Tournament Lanes.

1907   May Sutton wins the Wimbledon singles championship
        again.

        Birdie Humphreys is a medal winner for the second
        year in a row in special events held on the ABC Tour-
        nament Lanes.

1908   Although the IVth Olympiad provides "official" competi-
        tion for women in figure skating, gymnastics, and
        swimming and diving, the American Olympic Committee
        refuses to permit its female athletes to enter the events.
        "In other words, the Committee was opposed to women
        taking part in any activity in which they could not
        wear long skirts" (New York Times, quoted in Daven-
        port 1978, 58).

        After five unsuccessful attempts, Annie Peck Smith
        climbs the 22,205-foot peak of Mt. Huascaran in Peru--
        the highest climb in the Western Hemisphere to date.

1909   Hazel Hotchkiss wins the U.S. singles and doubles
        tennis tournaments.

1910   Hazel Hotchkiss wins the American singles and doubles
        tennis titles for the second year in a row.

1911   Harriet Quimby, the first American aviatrix, is granted
        her pilot's license.

        Hazel Hotchkiss wins her third straight American sin-
        gles and doubles titles.

        Marie Warmbier sets an all-events women's bowling
        record that will stand until 1959.

        Addie Ruschmeyer wins her first bowling trophy.

        Kate Sandwina lifts 286 pounds, a record that will
        stand until 1985.

1912   Harriet Quimby makes a successful flight over the

English Channel, but the news of her achievement is overshadowed by the sinking of the Titanic.

Fifty-seven women enter the Vth Olympiad in Stockholm. The American Olympic Committee still refuses to permit its female athletes to participate.

May Sutton Bundy becomes the clay court tennis champion in the United States.

1916   Olga Dorfner takes the national swimming title in the 50-yard freestyle.

Claire Galligan becomes the first Amateur Athletic Union (AAU) Women's National Swim Champion by winning the 500-yard freestyle in New York City.

The Women's International Bowling Congress (WIBC) is organized in St. Louis by Ellen Kelly (secretary), Gertrude Dornblasser (director), Catherine Menne (president), and 37 others.

II. THE ORGANIZATIONAL YEARS
1917-1956

1917   Elizabeth Burchenal takes over the chairmanship of
        Senda Berenson's group, which is now known as the
        Committee on Women's Athletics (CWA).

        Blanche Trilling of the University of Wisconsin organ-
        izes the Athletic Conference of American College Women
        (ACACW) in an effort to align women's athletic associa-
        tions with women's departments of physical education
        at American colleges and universities.

        Olga Dorfner wins the national 100-yard freestyle
        swimming title.

        The WIBC holds its first tournament in St. Louis.
        Almost 100 entrants are present.

        Grace Smith joins the first women's bowling league
        in Chicago, and goes on to record the highest average
        for Chicago women for 5 seasons. She will win a
        state and 5 city team championships in her career.

1918   Olga Dorfner wins national titles in both the 220- and
        440-yard freestyle events. She sets a world record
        for the 200-meter freestyle at Alameda, California,
        and is selected Swimmer of the Year in newspaper
        polls.

        Goldie Greenwald bowls in a men's league, averaging
        191 and rolling a 732 series, a high score for women
        at the time.

        Emma Jaeger wins the first of 9 WIBC championships.

1920   The Nineteenth Amendment to the U.S. Constitution is
        enacted, giving American women the right to vote.

        Sixty-three women participate in the VIIth Olympiad in
        Antwerp, among whom are 15 American swimmers and
        2 American figure skaters.

        Ethelda Bleibtrey becomes the first American woman to
        win a gold medal in swimming for her victory in the
        100-meter freestyle.

        Irene Guest wins the silver medal in the 100-meter
        freestyle, and Clara Schroth takes the bronze.

        At the age of 14, Aileen Riggin is the first female
        Olympic springboard diving champion.

        Birdie Humphreys wins the singles and team champion-
        ships at the WIBC Tournament.

1921   Bessie Coleman becomes the first black internationally
        licensed pilot on record.

1922   Gertrude Ederle breaks 7 world records in the course
        of a single 500-meter swim at Brighton Beach.

        Ethel McGray of New York swims 440 yards in 6 minutes,
        24.4 seconds. She is the first woman in swimming his-
        tory to break a man's record.

        Betty Becker wins her first national springboard diving
        championship on the 3-meter board.

        Aileen Riggin makes the first slow-motion and under-
        water swimming and diving films for Grantland Rice.

        Annie Oakley breaks 100 clay targets at Pinehurst,
        North Carolina, despite a severe auto accident the
        previous year.

        Louise Stockdale wins the WIBC doubles championship
        in her first tournament.

1923   Lou Henry Hoover, wife of the president of the United
        States, organizes the initial meeting of the Women's
        Division of the National Amateur Athletic Federation.
        The group helps popularize the slogan, "A sport for
        every girl and every girl in a sport."

        Betty Becker wins the national 3-meter springboard
        diving championship for the second year in a row.

        Helen Wills defeats Molla Mallory at Forest Hills, New
        York, and becomes the U.S. women's singles tennis
        champion at the age of 18.

        Hazel Hotchkiss Wightman donates the trophy for the
        first international team tennis matches between British
        and American women.

        Deane Fritz wins the WIBC all-events title.

        Nora Kay plays with the runner-up team in the WIBC
        Tournament.

1924   The International Women's Sports Federation is formed
        to call attention to the athletic capabilities of women.
        The group conducts its own Olympiad, to which the
        United States, under the auspices of the AAU, sends
        a team.

        Sybil Bauer is the first woman to break an existing
        men's world record in Olympic backstroke competition,
        winning the 100-meter event with a time of 1 minute,
        23.3 seconds.

        Gertrude Ederle wins 3 medals for the United States
        at the VIIIth Olympiad: bronze in the 100- and 400-
        meter freestyle and gold as a member of the freestyle
        relay team.

        Martha Norelius beats Gertrude Ederle and wins the
        gold medal in the 400-meter freestyle event.

        Ethel Lackie wins the 100-meter freestyle competition
        and anchors the American 400-meter freestyle relay
        team.

At the age of 16, Florence Chambers of San Diego
finishes fourth in the 100-meter Olympic freestyle
competition.

Aileen Riggin becomes the first competitor in the history of the Olympic Games to win medals for both
swimming and diving. She places third in the 100-
meter backstroke and second in the springboard diving
competition.

Betty Becker wins the 3-meter diving title, as well
as the national championship from the 1-meter board.
She returns from the Olympics with 2 medals.

Caroline Smith wins the Olympic competition in platform
diving.

Hazel Hotchkiss Wightman wins an Olympic gold medal
in tennis.

Helen Wills Moody wins Olympic gold medals in singles
and doubles tennis events.

Jeannette Knepprath serves as secretary of the Wisconsin Women's Bowling Association (WBA) and begins her
36-year presidency of the WIBC.

Grace Smith and her team, Albert Pick & Co., win the
WIBC team title.

1925   In an effort to promote the Women's Swimming Association, Gertrude Ederle tries, but fails, to swim the
English Channel.

Grace Smith and her team, Estes Alibis (formerly Albert Pick & Co.), are the first team to win the WIBC
team title 2 years in a row.

Grayce Garwood Hatch is the WIBC all-events champion.

1926   Gertrude Ederle becomes the first woman to swim the
English Channel. Her time of 14 hours, 39 minutes
from France to England is a world record.

Aileen Riggin turns pro, plays the Hippodrome for 3
weeks, and tours with Gertrude Ederle 6 months after
her English Channel swim.

Betty Becker Pinkston wins the 3-meter National Diving
Championship at Tampa, Florida.

Helen Wills Moody is defeated by Suzanne Lenglen
of France before a standing-room-only crowd of 4,000
at the Carleton Club in Cannes. The 2 are recognized
as the greatest women tennis players of their era.

Emily Chapman is a member of the WIBC champion
team, Taylor Trunks.

Lela Brooks wins first place at the world championships
of speed skating.

On New Year's Eve, 16-year-old Faye Baird is part of
a spectacular surfing demonstration. She rides a wave
with movie flares in both hands, blazing a trail of light
to shore. The San Diego partygoers who witness
her ride are astounded.

1927   Eleanor Holm wins the first of 9 national swimming
gold medals in the individual medley.

Glenna Collett refuses $50,000 a year to play profes-
sional golf, saying that she plays for pleasure, not
for money.

Bowler Floretta McCutcheon competes against ABC
Hall of Famer Jimmy Smith. The 39-year-old Mrs.
McCutcheon wins the match, 704-697.

Emma Phaler begins her term of office as WIBC executive secretary, which will last until 1965. The membership will increase during this period to nearly 2.7
million members in over 2,700 local associations.

Madalene "Bee" Hochstadter captains the Boyle Valves
to the WIBC team title.

Grayce Garwood Hatch is the WIBC all-events champion
for the second time in her career.

Lottie Schoemmel sets records for women's rowing
in both fresh and salt water. She rows 32 miles at
Lake Champlain, New York, in 7 hours, 48 minutes--
and 30 miles in the Pacific Ocean in 11 hours, 29 minutes.

1928 Amelia Earhart is the first woman passenger to cross
the Atlantic Ocean by air.

At Amsterdam, 290 women (121 of whom compete in
track and field) compete in the IXth Olympiad.

With a time of 1 minute, 11 seconds, Albina Osipowich
wins the 100-meter Olympic freestyle competition.

Martha Norelius wins the Olympic gold medal in the
400-meter freestyle event, becoming the first woman
to win successive gold medals in the Olympic Games.

Josephine McKin takes the bronze medal in the 400-
meter freestyle.

Genevieve Scully sets a Southern Pacific AAU record
of 3 minutes, 41 seconds in the 220-yard breaststroke.

Betty Becker Pinkston wins a second gold medal in
diving, taking first place in Olympic platform competition.

Helen Meany takes the gold medal in springboard diving competition.

Georgia Coleman places second on the platform and
second on the springboard in Olympic diving competition.

At the age of 13, Dorothy Poynton wins a bronze
medal for springboard diving.

Eleanora Sears wins the first women's squash racquets
championship. A Boston socialite, she is criticized
for her habits of wearing men's trousers and riding
horses astride. "Barriers mean nothing to her" (Howell 1982, 266) as she competes in a variety of sports

activities that include tennis, walking, sailing, golf,
polo, swimming, and trapshooting.

Elizabeth Robinson wins the Olympic gold medal in
the 100-meter dash.

The 800-meter Olympic dash for women is described
as a disaster: "Below us on the cinder path were
11 wretched women, five of whom dropped out before
the finish, while five collapsed after reaching the
tape.... The remaining starter fainted in the dress-
ing room shortly afterward" (Tunis, quoted in Davenport 1978, 59).

Jean Shiley of Harrisburg, Pennsylvania, places fourth
in Olympic high jump competition with a leap of 4
feet, 11 1/2 inches.

Lillian Copeland wins the silver medal in the discus
throw.

Anita Rump wins the WIBC singles championship.

1929   Martha Norelius, the Olympic swimmer, turns professional following her suspension from the AAU for swimming an exhibition in the same pool with professionals.

Leona Robinson is a member of the WIBC championship
team.

N. Marie Wardlow begins her pitching career, during
which she will win 341 games and lose only 51.   She
will pitch 42 no-hitters.

1930   The stated principles of women's athletics are (a)
the provision of opportunities for all; (b) the continu-
ation of the play activities of childhood; (c) the acqui-
sition of a lifelong love of activity; and (d) the social
development of individuals (Leslie 1979).

The New Jersey Athletic Commission bans a scheduled
boxing match between Mary Baxter and Sally Reneck.

The University of Southern California's polo team announces that it will not play UCLA unless Barbara
Rand, a member of the UCLA team, is replaced by a
man.

Helene Madison wins every freestyle swimming event
in the United States Women's Nationals for the first
of 3 consecutive years.

Aileen Riggin tours the world and helps organize Billy
Rose's first Aquacade.

Mildred "Babe" Didrikson wins her first national honors
at an AAU meet in Dallas. Her javelin and baseball
throws earn first-place titles, and her second-place
long jump betters a world record. Her nickname comes
from her ability to hit a baseball like Babe Ruth.

1931 Mabel Lee, premier physical educator and a "bloomer
girl" from the start, is elected the first woman president of the American Physical Education Association.

Amelia Earhart pilots her aircraft from Newfoundland
to Ireland, setting a world altitude record of 18,415
feet and becoming the first woman to fly solo across
the Atlantic Ocean.

Helene Madison, ranked as the greatest woman swimmer
of all time, shuns an offer of $17,500 to turn profes-
sional.

Babe Didrikson wins the 80-meter hurdle and long
jump competition at an AAU meet in Jersey City, New
Jersey. She throws a softball an unsurpassed 296
feet.

Mrs. J. E. Rankin wins the women's title in the first
National Open miniature golf tournament in Chattanooga,
Tennessee.

Emma Fahning becomes the first woman bowler to achieve
a perfect score in WIBC competition.

For the second time in her career, Anita Rump wins
the WIBC singles championship.

Myrtle Schulte captures the WIBC all-events championship.

Madalene "Bee" Hochstadter begins bowling in WIBC
tournaments. She will bowl in 46 tournaments in 38
consecutive years.

Philena Bohlen takes her team on a cross-country
exhibition. They bowl 37 matches in 49 days against
the best women's teams in 16 states.

Virne "Jackie" Mitchell becomes the first woman to
play for an all-male baseball team as she signs a contract to pitch for the Chattanooga Lookouts. In an
exhibition game against the New York Yankees on
April 2, she strikes out Babe Ruth and Lou Gehrig.

Jean Wilson wins first place at the North American
speed skating championships.

1932   Amelia Earhart flies 2,600 miles from Los Angeles to
Newark, New Jersey, in 19 hours, 5 minutes, becoming the first woman to complete a transcontinental
flight.

At the age of 82, Annie Peck Smith scales New Hamp-
shire's 5,363-foot Mt. Madison.

The CWA, the ACACW, and the Women's Division of
the National Amateur Athletic Federation all register
their disapproval of women's participation in the Olympic Games. The AAU stands alone in support of wom-
en's competition, and American women are permitted to
compete in the Xth Olympiad in Los Angeles.

Eleanor Holm wins the gold medal in the 100-meter
backstroke.

Helene Madison conquers all available swimming goals,
winning all the Olympic freestyle events, the National
Championship events, and the World Champion freestyle
events.

Georgia Coleman, the first woman to do a 2 1/2 forward

somersault in competition, wins the Olympic gold medal
in springboard diving and the silver medal in platform
diving.

Dorothy Poynton wins the gold medal in platform diving.

Lela Hall Frank wins the first of 9 straight Missouri
women's trapshooting titles. She captures 11 such
championships between 1932 and 1943, missing the
title only in 1941.

Helen Stephens competes on her high school's boys'
track team.

Lillian Copeland throws the discus a distance of 133
feet, 1 5/8 inches as she wins the Olympic gold medal.

Babe Didrikson wins Olympic gold medals in the 80-
meter hurdles and the javelin throw. Her record-
breaking effort in the high jump is disallowed because
of her failure to use the proper technique.

Using the proper technique, Jean Shiley wins the
gold medal for the high jump with a leap of 5 feet,
5 1/4 inches.

Evelyne Hall wins the silver medal in the 80-meter
hurdles.

Myrtle Schulte bowls with the WIBC championship team.

Beulah Abbott wins the International Women's Bowling
Association (IWBA) championships in Class A singles,
doubles, and all-events. Her all-events score of 1,761
will stand for 26 years.

In Olympic demonstration events, Jean Wilson is first
in the 500-meter and second in the 1500-meter speed
skating competition.

After the Olympic Games, Babe Didrikson tours the
United States, starring in such sports as track and
field, tennis, golf, basketball, diving, skating, and
lacrosse. She is named Female Athlete of the Year.

1933   Katherine Rawls breaks Eleanor Holm's world swimming
        record in the 300-yard individual medley with a time
        of 4 minutes, 14.4 seconds. She becomes the first
        woman to win 4 titles at the U.S. swimming champion-
        ships. In addition to the individual medley, she places
        first in the 200-meter breaststroke, the 880-yard free-
        style, and the springboard diving competition.

        Helen Wills Moody, world champion tennis player, de-
        feats Phil Neer before 3,000 fans, but sportswriters
        claim that she is not tested by a good male player.

        Traveling with Uncle Joe Thum's bowling team to Europe,
        Addie Ruschmeyer earns the women's international
        championship.

        Noel MacDonald begins a basketball career in which
        she will play 135 games and score 1,874 points, an
        average of 13.9 points per game.

1934   Genevieve Scully sets an outdoor record for San Diego
        County in the 220-yard breaststroke.

        Catherine Burling is a member of the WIBC champion-
        ship team.

        Violet "Billy" Simon captures the WIBC doubles title
        with Erna Haufler and averages 202 in league play.

        Esther Ryan wins the WIBC all-events title.

        Babe Didrikson pitches a full inning for the Philadelphia
        Athletics against the Brooklyn Dodgers without allowing
        a hit.

1935   Lela Hall Frank wins the first of four NACT champion-
        ships in trapshooting.

        Helen Stephens wins the 50-yard dash at the National
        AAU Women's Indoor Track Meet.

        During this year and the next, Marie Warmbier travels
        16,000 miles, giving exhibitions and challenging male

bowlers. She will carry an average above 190, roll
a 300 game, and shoot several 700 series.

1936 Expected to win the Olympic backstroke events, Eleanor
Holm is disqualified from the American team after sip-
ping champagne with shipboard officials en route to
the XIth Olympiad in Berlin.

Katherine Rawls wins the 100-meter freestyle event
in the Olympic trials, but must settle for the silver
medal in the competition. She also takes second place
in the springboard diving competition.

Marjorie Gestring of the United States wins the springboard diving competition at the age of 13.

Dorothy Poynton Hill takes the bronze medal in springboard diving and becomes the first woman to win 2
consecutive Olympic platform diving titles.

Velma Dunn places second in platform diving competition.

Mary Meadows wins the Grand American and Preliminary
Handicap titles in trapshooting.

Alice Marble wins her first U.S. Open women's singles
tennis championship.

Helen Stephens wins Olympic gold medals in the 100-
meter dash and the 400-meter relay. Her teammates
in the 400-meter relay are Elizabeth Robinson, Annette
J. Rogers, and Harriet Bland. Helen is selected Female Athlete of the Year in the United States.

Sally Stearns of Rollins College becomes the first woman
coxswain of a men's college varsity crew team.

1937 Amelia Earhart's plane goes down on her historic flight
around the world. The accident occurs over the Pacific
Ocean, between New Guinea and the Hawaiian Islands.

Eleanor Holm signs a contract to star in the Billy
Rose Aquacades. She marries her boss.

Mary Meadows begins a series of 11 Iowa State women's trapshooting championships.

Lela Hall Frank is first among women in yearly trap- shooting average. She becomes the first woman ever to lead her state in singles shooting.

With an error-free 1,761 total (including a 278 game), Louise Stockdale wins the WIBC all-events title.

Catherine Fellmeth competes with Chicago champions in bowling, softball, track, and basketball.

Ruth Sears begins her softball career with the Orange (California) Lionettes; her team will be named an Ama- teur Softball Association (ASA) All-American team 4 times.

The first sanctioned American championship bicycle race for women is won by Doris Kopsky.

The National Section on Women's Athletics (formerly the CWA) begins to recognize the competitive needs of highly skilled female athletes. Athletic competition can be valuable if programs conform to standards of common sense and good faith, it states.

1938 Dorothy Frazier wins the women's division of the Grand American Handicap (GAH) trapshooting competition.

Lela Hall Frank shoots a 98 in the GAH, a mark that will stand among women trapshooters for many years.

Alice Marble wins the U.S. Open women's singles tennis title for the second time.

Phyllis Wheeler wins the all-events title in IWBA compe- tition for the first of 2 consecutive years.

Floretta McCutcheon averages 206 in WIBC league play, a record that will stand until the 1952-53 season.

Ethel Sablatnik shares the WIBC doubles tournament title and is a member of the team that scores the highest series total in the nation.

Amy Peralta May begins a softball pitching career
in which she will compile a record of 447-79 and pitch
300 shutouts and 50 no-hitters.

1939   Esther Williams wins her first AAU championship in
the 100-meter freestyle.

Cleo Smiley sets a Far Western AAU swimming record
in the 200-meter breaststroke.   At 11 years of age,
she is the youngest ever to do so.

Eleanor Holm stars opposite Buster Crabbe and Johnny
Weissmuller at the New York World's Fair.

Mary Meadows becomes the only woman to win both
the Grand American and Preliminary Handicap trapshooting titles twice.

Seventeen-year-old Gloria Jacobs wins the National
Rifle Association (NRA) pistol championship with a
score of 299 out of 300, beating the 2-year-old record
of FBI agent Walter Walsh and becoming the first woman
to hold a world pistol mark.

Alice Marble wins another U.S. Open women's singles
tennis title.   She teams up with Sarah P. Fabyan
to win the doubles competition.

Esther Ryan and her Kornitz Pure Oil teammates win
the WIBC team title.

Connie Powers and Betty Reus win the WIBC doubles
title.

1940   Esther Williams is selected for the female lead opposite
Johnny Weissmuller in the San Francisco World's Fair
Aquacade.

The California Athletic Commission licenses Belle Martell
as the first female prizefight referee.

Tennis star Alice Marble wins her fourth U.S. Open
women's singles title and, with partner Sarah P. Fabyan,
her second doubles championship.   She turns professional

and signs for a tour, on which she will receive $25,000
plus a percentage of the gate.

Evelyn Boldrick Howard wins the National Women's
Singles Championship in badminton.

Tess Morris Small wins the WIBC tournament in 3 categories: team, doubles, and all-events.

1941   Alice Marble begins her professional tennis career
at Madison Square Garden, defeating Ruth Hardwick
of Great Britain.

Stella Hartrick earns a special award for her 620 series
at the WIBC tournament.

Nina Korgan hurls the Higgins Midgets of Tulsa, Oklahoma, to a National ASA title.

Anna Lee Wiley makes her debut as a professional
jockey in the Roamer Handicap in Mexico and becomes
the first woman to ride on a recognized track as a
licensed jockey.

1942   Evelyn Boldrick Howard wins her second National Wom-
en's Singles Championship in badminton and the doubles
title as well.

Stella Hartrick and Clara Allen win the WIBC doubles
title.

Tess Morris Small and Nine Van Camp Burns are on
the WIBC championship team. Small has the best-of-
series score (663), and Burns wins the all-events
crown.

Peggy Angus is the California State Women's Bowling
Association singles champion.

Nina Korgan, pitching for the Jax Maids, helps her
team win the first of 3 national titles.

1943   Nine Van Camp Burns wins the all-events bowling

title for Chicago women with a record total of
1,920.

Champion bowler Sally Twyford stars in a film for
Columbia Pictures.

Betty Evans Grayson pitches in her first ASA tournament.

1944   Ann Curtis sets a world swimming record in the 880-
yard race, and wins all 4 individual freestyle events
(100-, 400-, 800-, and 1500-meters) at the National
Outdoor Swimming Championships for Women. She is
the first woman to receive the James E. Sullivan Memorial Trophy, which is given by the AAU to the
amateur athlete who does the most to advance the
cause of good sportsmanship during the year.

Dorothy Marker is the women's champion in the GAH
of trapshooting. She shares second place in the women's
Preliminary Handicap competition.

Jean Doyle and Margaret Varner are the national junior
girls' tennis doubles champions.

Babe Didrikson is allowed special entry to the Pasadena
Men's Golf Tournament.

1945   Dorothy Marker wins the GAH for women trapshooters
for the second year in a row.

Jean Doyle and Margaret Varner win their second
consecutive national girls' junior doubles tennis championship.

Betty Evans Grayson and her team, Erv Lind Florists,
finish fourth in the ASA tournament.

Amy Peralta May leads the world softball tournament
for women with a .577 batting average.

1946   Vickie Manalo wins the U.S. outdoor highboard diving
championship.

Frances King Garlington and her husband, Clyde,
win the husband-and-wife trapshooting championship
with a score of 190.

Val Mikiel wins the WIBC singles title.

Betty Evans Grayson's Erv Lind Florists finish third
in the ASA Tournament.

The Philadelphia Phillies make headlines when they
hire Edith Houghton, a former women's baseball star,
as a team scout.

1947   Ann Curtis sets a world record for the 440-yard swim.

Vickie Manalo Draves retains her U.S. highboard diving
crown.

Pat McCormick takes second place in the National Platform Diving competition, missing a spot on the 1948
Olympic team.

Mary Meadows places second in the Women's Champion
of Champions trapshooting competition.

Lela Hall Frank wins the Champion of Champions competition with a perfect score of 100 straight. She is
also the California women's trapshooting champion
for the first of 3 consecutive years.

Frances King Garlington is the runner-up in the Georgia
State 16-yard trapshooting competition when she breaks
189 out of 200.

Babe Didrikson Zaharias wins 16 straight victories in
golf, including the coveted British Women's Amateur
Golf Championship.

Esther Ryan and her Kornitz Pure Oil teammates win
the WIBC team title again.

1948   Ann Curtis wins the gold medal in the 400-meter swimming competition at the XIVth Olympiad. She is a

member of the victorious 800-meter freestyle relay
team, and finishes second in the 100-meter race.

Former national junior AAU champion Muriel Mellon
places seventh in Olympic 100-meter backstroke competition.

Vickie Manalo Draves retains her American outdoor
highboard diving title and wins the indoor 3-meter
diving championship. She also wins both the Olympic
springboard and platform gold medals in London.

Zoe Ann Olson takes the silver medal in springboard
diving competition.

Patty Elsener wins the bronze medal for platform diving.

Fencer Jan York Romary competes in her first Olympic
Games.

Frances King Garlington wins the Southern Zone Open
Handicap in trapshooting with a score of 97.

Hortense Wood Hardesty wins her first singles title
in trapshooting at the Utah women's singles competition.
She will go on to win 17 more championships in her
career.

Pat Canning Todd wins the U.S. tennis indoor singles
championship.

This year's Olympics offer 9 track and field events
for women--the most ever.

Alice Coachman takes the Olympic high jump title with
a record jump of 5 feet, 6 1/8 inches.

Merle Matthews wins the WIBC doubles crown with
Margaret Franklin.

Val Mikiel is named Bowling Writers Association of
America (BWAA) Bowler of the Year.

The Erv Lind Florists, still featuring pitcher Betty
Evans Grayson, host the world softball tournament
and capture second place.

Amy Peralta May and Marjorie Law are members of
the Phoenix Ramblers, national softball champions
this year and next. Law is named to the All-American
team for the first of 8 times.

Gretchen Fraser wins a silver medal in Alpine ski
competition in the Vth Winter Olympic Games at St.
Moritz, becoming America's first woman slalom champion
and the first American skier to win a medal.

1949   Pat McCormick wins her first big meet, taking first
place in the National Platform Diving Competition in
San Antonio, Texas.

Iva Pembridge Jarvis commences a successful trapshooting career that will find her winning 14 Kansas women's
singles championships and 4 men's titles. She will be
named to 12 consecutive all-American teams.

Maureen Connolly wins the National Girls' Tennis Championship at the age of 14.

Gertrude "Gussie" Moran wins the United States Lawn
Tennis Association (USLTA) indoor women's singles,
doubles, and mixed doubles championships, as well
as the hard court women's doubles crown.

Dr. Nell C. Jackson breaks the American record in
the 200-meter track competition. She also wins the
national AAU championships in the 200-meter run and
the 400-meter relay.

Marie Robie drives a golf ball 393 yards to score a
hole in one at the Furnace Brook Golf Club in Massachusetts.

Patty Berg wins the Tampa Women's Open Golf Tourna-
ment and ties the 72 medal-play record of 295 strokes.
She is elected the first president of the newly formed
Ladies Professional Golf Association (LPGA).

Catherine Fellmeth wins the WIBC all-events title.

Cecelia Winandy captures her first WIBC tournament title.

Val Mikiel is named BWAA Bowler of the Year for the second year in a row.

Kay Rich is selected to the ASA All-American team for the first of 6 consecutive softball seasons.

1950   Florence Chadwick breaks Gertrude Ederle's 24-year-old record by swimming the English Channel from Wissant, France, to Dover, England, in 13 hours, 20 minutes.

Pat McCormick defends her national platform diving title and also wins the 1- and 3-meter national spring-board championships.

Jean Lee is the first woman to win a world target championship in archery.

Frances King Garlington wins the Georgia 16-yard trapshooting championship, as well as the husband-and-wife competition, with her husband, Clyde. Frances is voted into the Georgia Athletic Hall of Fame, along with her friends Bobby Jones and Ty Cobb.

Iva Pembridge Jarvis captures one of her 39 trophies in GAH trapshooting competition.

Patsy Zellmer and partner Maureen Connolly win the national junior girls' doubles tennis championships in Philadelphia.

Babe Didrikson Zaharias scores 106 points in one basketball game; strikes out Joe DiMaggio; holds records in 5 different track events; and sets a one-year money record of $14,800 by winning 6 major golf tournaments. She is named Female Athlete of the Year for the fifth time.

The American Bowling Congress is fined by a superior court judge in Chicago for limiting its membership to white males. The WIBC ends its membership restrictions against nonwhites.

Pat Dryer leads women bowlers in the nation with a 200 average.

Marion Ladewig wins the all-events crown and is voted
BWAA Bowler of the Year for the first of 5 consecutive
seasons. In all, she will receive the title 9 times.

Playing for the Chicago Queens, a professional softball
team, Betty Evans Grayson compiles a record of 35-5.

In one of her greatest seasons, Bertha Tickey wins
65 of 73 games for the Orange (California) Lionettes.
She fans 795 batters in 513 innings, yields only 143
hits, and compiles a streak of 143 scoreless innings.
Her team wins the first of 11 national championships.

Margaret Dobson sets the record for the highest batting
average in national softball competition. Her record
will stand for 25 years.

Carolyn Thome Hart, a member of the ASA All-American
team, is the fourth leading hitter in the world softball
tournament with a .391 average.

1951   Florence Chadwick is the first woman to swim the
        English Channel from England to France. All previous
        efforts had been from France to England.

        Pat McCormick wins a gold medal in platform diving at
        the Pan American Games. She also wins all 5 national
        diving titles (2 indoors and 3 outdoors) in the United
        States.

        Frances King Garlington wins the Georgia State trap-
        shooting championship.

        Maureen Connolly, at the age of 16, becomes the young-
        est woman to win the U.S. singles championship in
        tennis.

        Dr. Nell C. Jackson wins a gold medal in the 400-
        meter relay and a silver in the 200-meter race at the
        Pan American Games.

        Babe Didrikson Zaharias is the first woman to win
        over $15,000 in golf. She is selected Woman Golfer
        of the Year by the LPGA and Woman Athlete of the

Year by the Associated Press. Because she also excels at swimming, diving, baseball, basketball, bowling, and track, a sportswriter asks, "Is there anything you don't play?" "Yeah," Babe replies. "Dolls."

Pat Dryer and her team win the WIBC championship.

Virginia Busick achieves a 20-10 pitching record as she strikes out 251 batters. She is chosen an ASA All-Star.

Connie Powers bowls a 987 4-game series in All-Star competition.

1952   Florence Chadwick is the first woman to swim the Catalina Channel, setting a new overall men's and women's record.

Pat McCormick wins gold medals in the platform and springboard diving competitions at the XVth Olympiad in Helsinki. During her career, she will win 77 national diving championships.

Jan York Romary competes in her second Olympic foil fencing events.

Frances King Garlington wins the Georgia State trap-shooting championship.

Lela Hall Frank is the runner-up in the California trapshooting competition for women.

Mary Meadows captures the Amateur Trapshooting Association (ATA) Central Zone feminine singles trap-shooting title.

Maureen Connolly wins the singles titles at Wimbledon and the U.S. Open.

Mary Ann Eilenberger and Linda Mitchell team up to win the national junior girls' tennis doubles championship.

Pat Gallagher wins her first Mexico International Tournament in women's badminton.

AAU champion Heriwentha Mae Faggs leads the American 400-meter relay team to a gold medal in track.
Her teammates are Barbara Jones, Janet Morreau,
and Catherine Hardy.

Marjorie Larney of Brooklyn, New York, wins the
javelin throw in AAU competition with a toss of 126
feet, 3 7/8 inches. She makes the Olympic team,
but places only 13th in the competition.

Patty Berg shoots a 64 in 18 holes, a women's record
that will stand for 18 years, at a golf course in Richmond, California.

Phyllis Notaro rolls a record 289 game in the WIBC
tournament.

Martha Hoffman shares the WIBC doubles title.

Margaret Dobson handles 41 chances at third base
in national softball competition without an error.

Tenley Albright wins the U.S. figure skating championship for the first of 5 consecutive years.

Andrea Mead Lawrence wins Olympic gold medals in
the women's giant slalom and women's slalom competitions.

Patricia McCormick, the first woman professional North
American bullfighter, makes her brave debut in Ciudad
Juarez, Mexico.

1953 Florence Chadwick swims the English Channel from
England to France in 14 hours, 42 minutes, setting
a new women's record. She also swims the Straits
of Gibraltar--for a new men's and women's record--
and the Bosporus and the Dardanelles.

Punkin Flock begins a career of trapshooting success
with a runner-up trophy in the clay target championships of the GAH.

Hortense Wood Hardesty finishes second at the Utah
trapshooting championships.

Iva Pembridge Jarvis wins her first Champion of Champions trophy in the ATA.   She will win 3 other ATA titles.

Lela Hall Frank wins her 15th state championship, taking the women's trapshooting title in California.

Maureen Connolly wins the singles title at Wimbledon for the second consecutive year and the U.S. Open championship for the third consecutive year.   "Little Mo" adds the French International and Australian National titles to her list, becoming the first woman to win the "grand slam" of tennis.

Mary Ann Eilenberger is the national junior girls' tennis champion.   With her partner Nancy Dwyer, she also wins the national junior girls' doubles competition.

Pat Dryer and her bowling partner win the Bowling Proprietors' Association of America (BPAA) doubles crown.

Grayce Garwood Hatch, Goldie Greenwald, Emma Jaeger, Louise Stockdale, and Marie Warmbier are elected to the WIBC Hall of Fame.

Softball great Margaret Dobson is selected by the Portland, Oregon, sportswriters and broadcasters as one of the outstanding athletes of 1952.

Dorothy Wilkinson bats .363 during the regular softball season.

Kay Rich has an impressive season batting average of .370; she bats .333 in the national softball tournament.

Ruth Sears bats .343 in the ASA championship tournament.

Led by the pitching of Virginia Busick, the Fresno Rockets win the first of 3 national softball titles.

Jeanne Contel is named to the ASA All-American team for the first of 5 softball seasons.

Tenley Albright wins her second U.S. figure skating title and the world figure skating championship as well.

1954   Punkin Flock is named to the second women's all-American trapshooting team.

Iva Pembridge Jarvis shoots 200 at the Texas State trapshooting competition.

Maureen Connolly is the women's singles champion at Wimbledon for the third consecutive year.

Patty Berg is the leading money winner in the LPGA.

Babe Didrikson Zaharias makes one of the greatest comebacks in sports as she wins the U.S. Women's Open golf tournament less than one year after a cancer operation.

Olga Gloor bowls with the WIBC champion team, the Marhoefer Weiners.

Vera Schlenker bowls on the winning IWBA team and wins the Match Game Championships.

Dorothy Miller is elected to the WIBC Hall of Fame.

Pat Walker begins a 15-year softball career with the Orlando Rebels, during which she will bat .314 and steal 172 bases, both team records.

Jean Daves pitches for the Orlando Rebels for the first of 18 seasons. She will pitch 41 no-hitters and 197 shutouts, strike out 2,944 batters in 2,310 innings, and compile an earned run average of 0.39, while winning 255 games and losing only 59.

Dorothy Wilkinson bats .455 and achieves a fielding percentage of .988 on 84 chances.

Carol Spanks leads the league in hitting for the first of 5 times in her career.

Kay Rich is named Most Valuable Player in the national

softball tournament, hitting .316 and making only 2
errors.

Tenley Albright takes her third consecutive U.S.
figure skating title.

1955   Florence Chadwick swims the Channel from England
to France, setting a new world record: 13 hours,
55 minutes.

Pat McCormick wins gold medals in both platform and
springboard diving at the Pan American Games in
Mexico City.

Mary Meadows places third in the women's Champion
of Champions trapshooting competition. She also captures her second ATA Central Zone feminine singles
crown.

Hortense Wood Hardesty takes the all-around trapshooting title in Utah. She also breaks 192, the top score
of the day, in the GAH. She heads the women's Class
A standings for the ATA singles championship.

Patty Berg is the leading money winner in the LPGA
for the second year in a row.

Marion Ladewig wins the all-events crown in bowling
for the second time.

Helen Shablis wins the BPAA doubles title with Dorothy
Aldred.

Sylvia Wene Martin is a PBAA All-Star and BWAA
Bowler of the Year.

Shirley Garms captains the WIBC champion team.

Philena Bohlen is elected to the WIBC Hall of Fame.

Pat Walker bats her career high of .431 during the
softball season.

Kay Rich bats .611 in the national softball championships,
after batting .311 during the regular season.

Gloria May bats .444 in the national softball tournament and handles 42 fielding chances with only one error.

Dorothy Wilkinson bats .450 in the world softball tournament.

Estelle Caito begins a 10-year softball career, during which she will make only 57 errors, record 747 assists, make 728 putouts, and achieve a fielding percentage of .960. Her team, the Orange Lionettes, wins the national title for the first of 3 seasons.

Tenley Albright wins another U.S. figure skating championship.

1956   In response to expressed concern about the strength of Russian female athletes, U.S. Olympic Manager Roxanne Anderson states, "American women are not cream puffs."

Shelly Mann wins the gold medal in the 100-meter butterfly at the XVIth Olympiad in Melbourne.

Pat McCormick defends her platform and springboard diving titles, thus becoming the only person to win 4 gold medals in Olympic diving. She is the second woman to win the James E. Sullivan Memorial Trophy.

Fencer Jan York Romary competes in her third Olympic Games.

Iva Pembridge Jarvis shoots 200 at both the Golden West Grand and the GAH trapshooting competitions.

Tennis star Maureen Connolly Brinker is honored by her hometown and elected to the San Diego Hall of Champions.

Dr. Nell C. Jackson coaches the U.S. Olympic track and field teams.

At the age of 16, Wilma Rudolph, who had been unable to walk because of illness until the age of 8, becomes a member of the U.S. Olympic team. Her 400-meter

relay team takes the bronze medal for the United
States.

With an American and Olympic record jump of 5 feet,
9 1/4 inches, Mildred L. McDaniel wins the Olympic
high jump competition.

Vera Schlenker is one winner of the Class A doubles
IWBA competition. She also wins the singles and all-
events titles, enabling her to win all four Class A
championships during her bowling career.

Elvira Toepfer and Anita Cantaline win the BPAA doubles title.

Anita Cantaline earns the BPAA All-Star title and
is named BPAA Bowler of the Year.

Floretta McCutcheon is named to the WIBC Hall of Fame.

Jeanne Contel hits .333 in the national softball tournament.

Kay Rich and Gloria May are selected to the ASA All-
American second team for the first of 2 seasons.

Estelle Caito is named to the ASA All-American first
team for the first of 3 seasons.

Carol Heiss qualifies as the youngest member of the
U.S. Olympic skating team after finishing fourth in
the World Figure Skating Championships. A tendon
injury, however, eliminates her chances for an Olympic
victory.

Tenley Albright, the U.S. figure skating champion
for the fifth year in a row, takes the gold medal in
Olympic figure skating competition.

As a candidate for the Olympic ski team, Jill Kinmont
suffers a tragic skiing accident that severs her spinal
cord, leaving her paralyzed from the neck down. De-
termined to overcome disaster and achieve both physical
and financial independence, Jill struggles to learn to
write again. She will eventually complete college and
become a licensed teacher.

III. THE COMPETITIVE PERIOD
1957-1971

1957   The Division for Girls and Women's Sports (DGWS)
acknowledges that intercollegiate athletic programs
for women are acceptable if they are outgrowths of
solid curricular and intramural sports programs.

Chris von Saltza wins her first U.S. outdoor title in
the 220-yard backstroke at the age of 13.

Pat McCormick, Olympic diving champion, receives
the Babe Didrikson Zaharias Trophy as the outstanding female athlete of the year.

Punkin Flock tops women's singles scoring in the Southern Zone ATA Championship for the first of 9 consecutive years.

Frances King Garlington once again wins the women's
GAH in trapshooting.

At the age of 19, Althea Gibson is the first black to
win a Wimbledon singles title.

Karen Hantze of San Diego wins her first U.S. junior
girls' tennis title at the age of 14. She teams up
with Kathy Chabot to win the national 15-and-under
doubles championship.

Marjorie Larney sets an AAU and national record in
the javelin throw: 187 feet, 8 inches.

Patty Berg is the leading money winner in the LPGA
for the third time in her career.

34

Gloria May is selected to the ASA All-American first softball team for the second of 3 times in her career.

Virginia Busick is selected to the ASA All-Star team.

Dorothy Wilkinson bats .387 in the World Softball Tournament.

Amy Peralta May and N. Marie Wardlow are elected to the National Softball Hall of Fame.

Anita Cantaline wins the WIBC all-events crown and the WIBC team title.

Ann Rand is a member of the Class A championship team in the IWBA for the fourth time in her career.

Carol Heiss wins the U.S. and world figure skating championships.

1958   Punkin Flock leads the women in scoring at the Vandalia Trapshooting Handicap. She also wins the Grand American doubles championship.

Billie Jean Moffitt wins her first tennis singles tournament.

Althea Gibson takes the women's singles title at Wimbledon for the second consecutive year.

Mary Kathryn "Mickey" Wright wins her first U.S. Open Golf Tournament and her first LPGA national title.

Ann Rand breaks the IWBA all-events record set in 1932 with a score of 1,819.

Cecelia Winandy and Mae Bolt are members of the WIBC Champion Allgauer's Restaurant team. The Chicago group will go on to win 3 more championships.

Elvira Toepfer finishes second in the World Invitational Bowling Doubles Tournament by 3 pins. She also finishes fourth in the all-star competition.

Catherine Burling is elected to the WIBC Hall of Fame.

Iolia Lasher is accorded WIBC member-emeritus status.

Mickey Stratton begins a series of 7 years during
which she will be elected to the ASA All-American
first team 5 times and the second team twice.

At the age of 18, Kathy Kusner establishes a world
record in women's equestrian jumping, clearing a height
of 7 feet, 3 inches.

Carol Heiss wins her second consecutive gold medals
in figure skating at both the U.S. championships and
the World Championship Games.

1959   Swimmer Chris von Saltza of the United States wins
5 gold medals at the Pan American Games. This is
the climax of a year in which she has broken 75 American records for 17 different distances in the backstroke,
freestyle, and individual medley events.

On October 1, Carol Chaplin swims from the Coronado
Islands to Point Loma, California (a distance of 22
miles), in 13 hours, 26 minutes, 17 seconds.

Punkin Flock is the runner-up in the Grand American
doubles championship of trapshooting. Between now
and 1972, she will lead all women in number of doubles
targets shot 8 times.

Dorothy Marker is the runner-up in the Women's Champion of Champions trapshooting competition.

Iva Pembridge Jarvis wins the twin-bird title at the
Golden West Grand trapshooting competition.

Althea Gibson is signed for a professional exhibition
tennis tour with the Harlem Globetrotters basketball
team.

Kathy Chabot and Karen Hantze of San Diego team
up to win the national junior girls' tennis doubles
title.

Pat Gallagher wins badminton singles titles in the
Mexico International and Pacific Southwest Open tournaments.

Marjorie Larney wins the silver medal in the javelin
throw at the Pan American Games.

Mickey Wright wins her second consecutive U.S. Open
Golf Championship.

Anita Cantaline and Elvira Toepfer lead their bowling
team to its second WIBC championship.

Olga Gloor captures the World Invitational bowling
title and helps organize the Professional Women Bowlers Association (PWBA).

Jo Mraz is elected to the WIBC Hall of Fame.

Betty Evans Grayson is elected to the National ASA
Hall of Fame.

Kathryn King hits a home run over the scoreboard
at Raybestos Memorial Field in Stratford, Connecticut,
becoming the first woman to accomplish this feat. She
is named to the ASA All-American first team for the
first of 4 seasons.

Carol Heiss wins her third consecutive gold medals
in figure skating at the U.S. championships and the
World Championship Games.

1960 Florence Chadwick makes her last long-distance swim.

Donna deVarona is the youngest member of the American team for the XVIIth Olympiad.

Lynn Burke takes the Olympic gold medal in the 100-
meter backstroke.

With a time of 1 minute, 9.5 seconds, Carolyn Schuler
wins the gold medal in the 100-meter butterfly competition.

Chris von Saltza wins 1 silver and 3 gold medals at
the Olympic Games in Rome. She sets a world record
for the 400-meter freestyle, ending Australian domination of that event, and is chosen the outstanding
female swimmer of the Games.

Jan York Romary competes in the foil fencing events
at the Olympic Games.

For the first of 3 consecutive years, Dorothy Marker
registers the most singles targets among women trapshooters.

Mary Meadows wins her third and final crown in the
ATA Central Zone women's singles competition.

Hortense Wood Hardesty is the women's ATA doubles
average leader. She is elected president of the Salt
Lake Gun Club, becoming the first woman to head a
major gun club.

Iva Pembridge Jarvis shoots another 200 at the Kansas
Western Zone trapshooting competition.

Patty Barth teams up with Margaret Taylor to win
the national girls' 15 doubles championship in tennis.
Patty also takes the Western Open and Pacific Southwest girls' 15 singles titles.

Kathy Chabot and Karen Hantze win their third national junior girls' doubles crown.

Badminton star Pat Gallagher wins the women's singles
competition in the Southern California, Mexico International, Western State Open, and Pacific Southwest
Open tournaments.

Wilma Rudolph becomes the first woman to win 3 gold
medals in Olympic track events. She takes the 100-
and 200-meter dashes and anchors the American wom-
en's 400-meter relay team.

Track star Mamie Rollins races over the 70-yard low
hurdles in 8.7 seconds, setting a record for women.

Olga Connolly, a Czechoslovakian gold-medal-winning discus thrower in 1956, represents the United States in the Olympic Games after her marriage to Harold Connolly.

At the Memphis Women's Open Golf Tournament, Mickey Wright sets the LPGA 72-hole tournament record and wins the tournament for the second time. Her stroke average is 73.25 for the year.

Shirley Garms is recognized as Chicago's Bowler of the Decade.

Jeannette Knepprath is accorded life-member status in the WIBC.

D. D. Jacobson wins her first national BPAA team title.

Violet (Billy) Simon is elected to the WIBC Hall of Fame. Her accomplishments include an all-events, a singles, and 2 doubles titles.

Sylvia Wene Martin wins the PBAA all-star competition and is named BWAA Bowler of the Year for the second time.

Ruth Sears and Nina Korgan are elected to the National Softball Hall of Fame.

Estelle Caito bats .381 in the national softball tournament.

Shirley Topley is named to the second all-American softball team for the first of 6 seasons.

Carol Heiss wins the gold medal for figure skating at the Olympic Games. She also wins the U.S. and world championship titles for the fourth consecutive year.

Betsy Snite wins a silver medal in Olympic downhill slalom competition.

Penny Pitou wins 2 silver medals in Olympic skiing:

one in the giant slalom and the other in downhill competition.

1961   Olympic gold medal winner Wilma Rudolph is named
       Female Athlete of the Year for the second time by
       the Associated Press. She becomes the third woman
       ever to win the coveted Sullivan Memorial Trophy
       for outstanding performance by an amateur athlete.

       Hortense Wood Hardesty is tops in the singles class
       in trapshooting competition for the second time in
       her career.

       Dorothy Marker places second in the women's H.O.A.
       standings at the Grand American Trapshooting compe-
       tition. With her husband, Van, she sets a new record.
       Never before have a husband and wife had perfect
       scores in the same event at the Grand American com-
       petition.

       Karen Hantze, 18, and Billie Jean Moffitt, 17, are
       the youngest team to win the women's doubles title
       at Wimbledon.

       Pat Gallagher is the badminton champion of the state
       of California. She also wins the Pacific Southwest
       Open tournament.

       Mickey Wright sets a new record on the golf circuit,
       winning a total of 10 tournaments, among them the
       prestigious "triple": the LPGA, the U.S. Open, and
       the Titleholders Tournament. She is the leading LPGA
       money winner with a total of $22,236.

       Louise Suggs outplays 10 male golfers in a par-3 invi-
       tational tournament at Palm Beach. She takes advantage
       of the short course (where the average distance between
       tee and flag is just under 150 yards), shooting 156 for
       54 holes. She beats Sam Snead by 2 strokes. Patty
       Berg, the only other woman in the competition, places
       last with 167.

       Shirley Garms is named Bowler of the Year.

Sylvia Wene Martin is selected Pennsylvania's Sportswoman of the Year.

Helen Duval wins the BPAA doubles title with Nobu
Asami.

Mae Bolt and friends win their second WIBC team championship, representing Allgauer's Fireside Restaurant.

Marge Merrick defeats Marion Ladewig to win the World
Invitational trophy in bowling.

Dorothea Fort is the IWBA Class A all-events champion.

Dorothy Miller is named the Quarter Century Club's
Bowler of the Year.

Addie Ruschmeyer is elected to the WIBC Hall of Fame.

Norma Eschenbrenner Ante hits .602, her highest
batting average, in national tournament play.

Shirley Topley is named to the first all-American softball team for the first of 9 seasons.

Judy Dibble wins the Women's Unlimited Division title
in the West Coast Surfing Championships.

1962 Swimmer Florence Chadwick is inducted into the San
Diego Hall of Champions.

Frances King Garlington finally wins the Champion
of Champions trapshooting competition, having tied
for the title 6 times.

Punkin Flock tops the women's scoring in her class in
the Grand American singles competition. She is the
runner-up for the doubles championship.

Dorothy Marker pulls the trigger on her 100,000th
target, becoming the first woman in ATA history to
achieve that goal.

Karen Hantze Susman captures the singles championship

at Wimbledon. She and Billie Jean Moffitt win another Wimbledon women's doubles title.

Pat Gallagher wins another Mexico International Tournament in women's badminton singles.

Mickey Wright is elected to the Women's Golf Hall of Fame and the San Diego Hall of Champions. So far, she has won 82 LPGA tournaments, 4 LPGA national titles, 4 U.S. Women's Open titles, and 5 consecutive Vare Trophies for having the lowest scoring average. In Midland, Texas, she sets an LPGA record with a score of 62. She is the top LPGA money winner for the second year in a row, this time with a total of $21,641.

Marge Merrick wins all-American honors from Bowler's Journal and Bowling Illustrated.

Martha Hoffman wins the WIBC singles competition. She also shoots a tournament record 296, which will remain unbeaten until 1979.

Betty Kuczynski and Joy Abel win the BPAA doubles tournament.

Merle Matthews captains the Linbrook Bowl team to the WIBC championship.

Shirley Garms wins the BPAA All-Star Tournament and retains her Bowler of the Year title.

Anita Rump is elected to the WIBC Hall of Fame.

Softball pitcher Joan Joyce throws over 30 pitches to Ted Williams of the Boston Red Sox. The .400 hitter manages to hit only a couple of weak foul balls.

Pat Walker steals a career-high 21 bases during the softball season.

Norma Eschenbrenner Ante and Alberta Kohls Sims are among the members of Dana Garden, the national champion slow-pitch softball team. As the team wins 3 consecutive titles, Sims will also be selected to the all-American team 3 times.

In recognition of her softball accomplishments, Margaret Dobson is elected to the Portland Hall of Fame.

Judy Dibble wins her second consecutive Women's Unlimited Division West Coast Surfing Championship.

1963   The DGWS changes its attitude about women's athletics, stating in its annual publication that competitive opportunities beyond the intramural program are desirable and should be provided for highly skilled women.

The first National Institute on Girls' Sports is founded at the University of Oklahoma.

Frances King Garlington makes her final appearance in trapshooting, winning the Peach State women's championship for the 20th time.

Lela Hall Frank wins her 16th and final California state trapshooting title.

Punkin Flock triumphs over her competitors in the Champion of Champions trapshooting competition for women.

Dorothy Marker is the runner-up in the Grand American doubles trapshooting competition.

Fran Davenport throws the javelin 168 feet, 8.3 inches at the international competition in Mainz, Germany. The AAU champion is the first American to win a javelin competition in Europe.

Edith McGuire, AAU champion in the 100-meter dash, wins the gold medal at the Pan American Games with a record-tying time of 11.5 seconds.

Mickey Wright sets an LPGA record with 13 tournament victories in a single year. She wins the most money for the year in LPGA competition. Her total of $31,269 is almost $10,000 more than her 1962 total.

Jeannette Knepprath is elected to the WIBC Hall of Fame, as is Esther Ryan.

Beulah Abbott and Phyllis Wheeler are elected to the
IWBA Hall of Fame.

Bowler Judy Soutar receives the Alberta E. Crowe
Star of Tomorrow Award.

Sylvia Wene Martin is named Philadelphia's Outstanding Athlete.

Merle Matthews captains the Linbrook Bowl team to
its second consecutive WIBC championship.

Marion Ladewig wins the BPAA All-Star and World
Invitational competitions.

Shirley Topley wins the batting title for the Raybestos
Brakettes with a .372 average.

Jeanne Contel hits .375 in the national softball tournament.

Norma Eschenbrenner Ante is named to the all-American
softball team for the first of 3 seasons.

Kay Rich is elected to the National ASA Hall of Fame.

Linda Benson, U.S. girls' champion, receives the
Surfer Poll Award for the best woman surfer.

1964   At the XVIIIth Olympiad, Donna deVarona wins two
       gold medals in swimming. She is voted America's
       Outstanding Woman Athlete and Outstanding Female
       Swimmer, as well as San Francisco's Outstanding Woman
       of the Year. She also receives awards from Mademoi-
       selle and the National Academy of Sports.

       Cathy Ferguson of Burbank, California, a product
       of the American age-group competitive swimming pro-
       gram, defeats 5 world-record-breakers to win the
       Olympic gold medal in the 100-meter backstroke.

       Fifteen-year-old Sharon Stouder wins the Olympic
       100-meter butterfly and the freestyle and medley re-
       lays. She takes second place in the 100-meter freestyle.

Virginia Duenkel wins the 400-meter Olympic freestyle competition with a time of 4 minutes, 43.3 seconds.

Lesley Bush wins the gold medal in the Olympic platform diving competition.

Foil fencer Jan York Romary competes in her fifth Olympic Games.

Diane Vetrecin wins the national women's amateur freestyle field archery title.

Billie Jean Moffitt and Karen Hantze Susman team up to win the women's doubles competition at the U.S. Open tennis championships. For Karen, it is her 17th national tennis title.

Pat Gallagher is the Southern California women's singles badminton champion. She also wins her fifth Mexico International Tournament.

Wyomia Tyus wins her first Olympic gold medal in the 100-meter dash.

Edith McGuire wins the 200-meter race in 23.0 seconds. She takes second place in the 100-meter dash.

Olga Connolly throws the discus for the United States in the Olympic Games.

Marian E. Washington is the Middle Atlantic AAU champion in both the discus and shotput competitions.

In the Tall City Open Golf Tournament for women, Mickey Wright shoots a 62 on a course where the men's record is 66. She wins the U.S. Women's Open and is named Woman Athlete of the Year for the second year in a row. She takes her fourth consecutive first place among LPGA money winners.

Betsy Peeney wins top honors in the Women's Division of the All-Navy Golf Tournament held at the Naval Air Station, Oak Harbor, Washington.

Joanne Chapman and LaVina Head set a doubles record in bowling with a score of 1,312.

Joan Holm sets a WBA all-events record with a score of 1,920.

Shirley Garms and Grace Werkmeister win the WIBC doubles trophy. Garms is second to D. D. Jacobson in the WIBC Queens Tournament.

Betty Kuczynski and Joy Abel win the BPAA doubles tournament. Kuczynski also wins the pro championship competition.

Mae Bolt and the Allgauer's Fireside Restaurant team win their third WIBC championship.

LaVerne Carter wins the BPAA All-Star title and is named BPAA Bowler of the Year.

Donna Zimmerman wins the PWBA title.

Lo Borschuk receives the National Women Bowling Writers' AMF Helen Duval Award for outstanding service.

Nora Kay, Marion Ladewig, and Sally Twyford are elected to the WIBC Hall of Fame. Ladewig also receives the Flowers for the Living Award.

Shirley Topley wins a second batting title for the Raybestos Brakettes, compiling an average of .340.

Alberta Kohls Sims is named Most Valuable Player in the all-American softball game.

Margaret Dobson is elected to the ASA Hall of Fame.

Paula Murphy sets a world land-speed record for women--226.37 miles per hour--on the Bonneville Salt Flats of Utah. Her car is the "Avenger," a 10,000-horsepower model.

Peggy Fleming wins her first U.S. figure skating championship.

Joyce Hoffman receives the Surfer Poll Award as the best woman surfer.

1965   Synchronized swimmer Pam Morris is the first triple
       winner in her sport, taking the solo, duet, and team
       titles in the championships held at Houston, Texas,
       and Maumee, Ohio.

       The Swimming Hall of Fame inducts its first 21 honorees
       in Fort Lauderdale, Florida. Among the inductees are
       Gertrude Ederle, Pam Morris, Katherine Rawls, and
       Pat McCormick.

       Donna deVarona is recognized as the Queen of Swimming
       by the International Swimming Hall of Fame at its first
       meet.

       Diane Vetrecin wins her second consecutive title in
       women's amateur freestyle field archery.

       Nancy Myrick wins the U.S. Nationals in archery,
       having taken up the sport only 2 years earlier.

       Punkin Flock takes AA honors in the singles class
       championship of trapshooting at the Grand American
       competition.

       Thirteen-year-old Patty Martinez becomes the youngest
       national champion in table tennis history, winning
       the national title, the girls' 15-and-under title, and
       the girls' 18-and-under title.

       Olympian Edith McGuire wins the AAU 200-meter race
       with a time of 23.6 seconds.

       Carol Mann wins the U.S. Women's Open golf tourna-
       ment.

       Kathy Whitworth leads women's golf in tournament
       wins and is named America's Outstanding Woman Athlete.

       Joan Holm leads the nation's women bowlers with a 207
       season average, the first average over 200 compiled by
       a Chicago woman. She bowls one perfect game during
       the season.

       Shirley Garms captains the WIBC championship team.

Betty Kuczynski wins the WIBC Queens title and is
named BPAA Bowler of the Year.

Donna Zimmerman wins the WIBC all-events title and
the BPAA doubles crown with Janet Harman. Zimmerman is also named to the Bowlers' Journal All-American
team and earns Southern California Bowler of the Year
honors.

Emma Phaler is accorded WIBC life-member status,
and is elected to the WIBC Hall of Fame with Myrtle
Schulte.

Pat Harrison scores 64 runs and hits 12 triples in
women's softball competition.

Jean Daves sets a new record of consecutive scoreless
innings pitched.

Donna Wolfe competes in the first of 12 national softball tournaments. She is named to the all-American
team for the first of 5 seasons.

Kathryn King represents the United States in the
first Women's World Fast Pitch Championships.

Lee Breedlove, driving her husband's car, sets a new
women's land-speed record of 308.6 miles per hour.

All eyes are glued on Peggy Fleming as she wins her
second national figure skating championship at Lake
Placid.

1966   The Commission on Intercollegiate Athletics for Women
       (CIAW) is organized by the DGWS. The purpose of
       the new group is to encourage intercollegiate athletic
       competition.

       Claudia Kolb of the United States sets a world swimming
       record in the 200-meter medley.

       "Pokey" Watson takes the U.S. outdoor titles in the
       100- and 200-meter freestyle swimming events.

This year's inductees into the Swimming Hall of Fame
include Ann Curtis, Eleanor Holm, Helene Madison,
Esther Williams, Shelly Mann, Chris von Saltza, and
Georgia Coleman.

Diane Vetrecin wins her third national title at the
Women's Amateur Freestyle Field Archery Championships.

After a 6-year layoff, Iva Pembridge Jarvis wins her
third clay target championship and her sixth doubles
championship and finishes third in the Grand American
Champion of Champions competition.

Billie Jean King wins her first Wimbledon singles crown.

Kathy Whitworth leads women's golf in tournament
wins and is named the Outstanding American Woman
Athlete for the second consecutive year.

Sylvia Wene Martin and Deane Fritz are elected to
the WIBC Hall of Fame.

Laura Albrecht is elected to the IWBA Hall of Fame.

Shirley Topley leads the Pacific Coast women's softball
league in hitting.

Pat Harrison leads her team in hitting and is named
to the first all-American softball team.

Jean Daves sets a new record for most shutouts in a
season (30), and wins a record 21 consecutive games.

Pat Walker is named to the first all-American team
for the first of 2 seasons.

Carolyn Thome Hart is elected to the National Softball
Hall of Fame.

Peggy Fleming wins her third consecutive national
figure skating championship. She is the world champion figure skater as well.

Waterskier Stephanie Stephens Shackelford wins the

American Water Ski Association Western Regional Overall women's title and the slalom event in the Tournament
of Champions.

1967   Catie Ball wins the 100- and 200-meter breaststroke
titles at the Pan American Games, as well as the U.S.
outdoor swimming crown.

Pan American 400- and 800-meter champion Debbie
Meyer is named Woman Athlete of the Year and World
Swimmer of the Year.

This year's inductees into the Swimming Hall of Fame
include Martha Norelius, Aileen Riggin, and Betty
Becker Pinkston, whose husband and coach, Clarence,
was previously so honored.

Nancy Myrick is the first woman in the world to score
over 1,200 points in archery.

Hortense Wood Hardesty wins the Utah doubles trapshooting competition and becomes the fifth woman in
the ATA to fire from the 25-yard line. Thirty-six
days later, she earns another yard and becomes the
fourth woman to fire from the 26-yard line.

Billie Jean King wins the women's singles and doubles
and mixed doubles competitions at Wimbledon. She
wins the U.S. Open women's singles and doubles titles
as well.

Judy Devlin Hashman wins unprecedented 12th national
titles in women's badminton singles and doubles competition.

Patty Martinez wins the women's singles title at the
U.S. National Table Tennis Championships. She is
also part of the winning women's and mixed doubles
teams.

Barbara Ferrell of Hattiesburg, Mississippi, wins a
gold medal in the 100-meter dash at the Pan American
Games.

Katherine Switzer is the first official woman entrant
in the Boston Marathon.

Kathy Whitworth leads women tournament golfers in
wins for the third consecutive year.

Mildred Martorella sets a WIBC record for the highest
season average with a 219.

Margaret Higley is voted WIBC member-emeritus status.

The WIBC Hall of Fame electees include Emily Chapman,
Iolia Lasher, and Madalene "Bee" Hochstadter.

Helen Weston of Detroit rolls a record 4,585 in 24
games at a bowling competition in Malmö, Sweden.

Mary Jo Peppler leads the American women's volleyball
team to victory at the Pan American Games.

Pat Walker bats .412 in national softball competition.

Jean Daves sets a new record for most strikeouts in a
season (485).   She also pitches a record 9 no-hitters.

Bertha Hickey hurls a perfect game against Houston
in national softball competition.

Softball is included as a demonstration event at the
Pan American Games in Winnipeg.   Kathryn King helps
represent the United States.

Kathy Kusner is denied a jockey license by the Mary-
land Racing Commission.

Peggy Fleming wins her fourth national figure skating
championship and her second consecutive world title.

Stephanie Stephens Shackelford is the national slalom
waterskiing champion and repeats her 1966 victories
in the American Water Ski Association Western Regional
Overall competition and the Tournament of Champions
slalom event.

1968   The DGWS stipulates in its statement of policy that the

holding of national collegiate athletic championships for
women will not detract from the effectiveness of instruc-
tional and intramural physical education programs.

Catie Ball wins the U.S. outdoor swimming title for
the second year in a row.

Debbie Meyer of Sacramento, California, wins 3 individual gold medals in the XIXth Olympiad and is named
World Swimmer of the Year. She is the fourth woman
to receive the Sullivan Memorial Trophy.

Claudia Kolb wins gold medals in the 200- and 400-
meter individual medleys and the 400-meter breaststroke.

Jan Henne takes the gold medal in the 100-meter freestyle competition with a time of 1 minute.

Kaye Hall wins the Olympic 100-meter backstroke competition.

With a time of 2 minutes, 44.4 seconds, Sharon Wich-
man wins a gold medal in the 200-meter breaststroke.

Although her previous titles were in freestyle competition, "Pokey" Watson breaks the world record in the
200-meter backstroke.

Sue Gossick takes the Olympic springboard diving
championship.

Dorothy Poynton Hill is named to the Swimming Hall
of Fame.

Diane Vetrecin wins her fourth national title in women's
amateur freestyle field archery.

Foil fencer Jan York Romary competes in her sixth
Olympic Games.

Punkin Flock is the third of 4 women in ATA history
to score 99 out of 100 in doubles competition at the
Florida State Trap Shoot.

Billie Jean King wins her third Wimbledon singles trophy in a row.

Valerie Ziegenfuss, a San Diego native, and partner Nancy Richey are the number one doubles team in women's tennis, according to a USLTA ranking.

Patti Hogan of La Jolla, California, wins the Southern California women's singles tennis title.

Patty Martinez takes first place in the women's singles, women's doubles, and mixed doubles competitions at the Canadian Table Tennis Championships.

Madeline Jackson-Manning becomes the first American woman to win an Olympic gold medal in the 800-meter running event. Her performance establishes a new world record: 2 minutes, 0.9 seconds.

Wyomia Tyus wins her second Olympic gold medal in the 100-meter dash with a time of 11.0 seconds. She is the only woman to win the 100-meter dash in two Olympiads.

Barbara Ferrell takes second place in the 100-meter dash and fourth place in the 200-meter run. She and Wyomia Tyus team up with Margaret Bailes and Mildrette Netter to win the gold medal in the 400-meter relay.

Patty Jean Johnson ties an Olympic record in the 100-meter hurdles, but places fourth in the competition.

Olga Connolly throws the discus for the United States in Olympic competition for the third time.

At the age of 16, Cathy Rigby is the smallest competitor at the Olympic Games. Weighing only 89 pounds, at a height of just over 4'1", she accumulates the highest score ever for an American woman gymnast.

Kathy Whitworth leads women's golf in tournament wins for the fourth consecutive year.

Susie Maxwell Berning wins the U.S. Women's Open golf tournament.

Beverly Ortner bowls 818 in a 3-game set and posts
a season average of 205. She is elected to the IWBA
Hall of Fame.

Dorothy Fothergill wins her first of two consecutive
BPAA all-star tournaments and is named Bowler of
the Year for the first of 2 years in a row.

Joanne Chapman wins the IWBA singles and the Sioux
City WBA all-events titles.

Bertha McBride is given WIBC member-emeritus status,
and is elected to the WIBC Hall of Fame with Grace
Smith.

The IWBA Hall of Fame electees include Ethel "Billy"
Lindelof (posthumously) and Lena McWade.

Mary Jo Peppler wins a spot on the American volleyball
team, but quits to turn professional after a dispute
with the organizers of the team.

In her final national softball tournament, Bertha Tickey
pitches a 13-inning no-hitter against a team from Fresno,
California.

Norma Eschenbrenner Ante helps Escue Pontiac capture
the women's slow-pitch softball national championship.

Pat Harrison is named to the first all-American softball
team for the second time in her career.

Kathy Kusner is the first woman to be granted a jockey
license.

Janet Lynn is the youngest skater eligible for the
U.S. Olympic team.

Peggy Fleming wins the Olympic gold medal in figure
skating. She also takes the U.S. and world figure
skating titles.

Waterskier Stephanie Stephens Shackelford wins the
American Water Ski Association Western Regional Overall
women's title and the slalom event in the Tournament
of Champions for the third year in a row.

Margo Godfrey Oberg dethrones Joyce Hoffman as
the U.S. surfing champion.

1969   The CIAW and the DGWS sponsor national intercollegiate
       championships for women in golf, gymnastics, and
       track and field.

       Debbie Meyer is named World Swimmer of the Year
       for the third year in a row.

       Heidi O'Rourke wins national AAU medals in the indoor
       and outdoor synchronized swimming events and is
       named to the all-American synchronized swimming team.

       Gail Johnson wins the team competition in synchronized
       swimming at the Canadian Nationals.

       The Swimming Hall of Fame inducts new members Donna
       deVarona and Vickie Manalo Draves.

       Seventeen-year-old Ruth White becomes the youngest
       national fencing champion and the first black woman
       to win a major American fencing title.

       Patti Hogan wins the Eastern Grass Courts singles
       title in women's tennis.

       Table tennis great Patty Martinez sweeps the American
       and Canadian table tennis championships, winning
       the women's singles, women's doubles, and mixed doubles
       trophies at both tournaments.

       Marian E. Washington is one of two black women to
       qualify for the American national track team.

       Madeline Jackson-Manning is named the Outstanding
       Athlete at the U.S.-European track meet.

       Donna Caponi wins the U.S. Women's Open golf tourna-
       ment.

       Kathy Whitworth leads women's tournament golf in
       victories for the fifth straight year.

Carol Mann is the leading LPGA money winner for
the year.

Joanne Chapman, Beverly Ortner, and Helen Duval
are all members of the WIBC champion Fitzpatrick
Chevrolet team. Duval also wins the all-events tournament title with a score of 1,927.

Judy Soutar and Gloria Simon win their first of 2
WIBC doubles titles. Their score of 1,315 is a new
record.

Laura Albrecht is elected WIBC member emeritus.

Inductees to the WIBC Hall of Fame include Leona
Robinson and Margaret Higley.

Floy Harmsen is elected to the IWBA Hall of Fame.

Bowler Ann Rand is elected to the Fort Dodge (Iowa)
Hall of Fame.

Shirley Topley is the first player to coach women's
softball.

Jeanne Contel and Mickey Stratton are chosen for
the National Softball Hall of Fame.

Diane Crump becomes the first woman jockey to ride
at a pari-mutuel race track in the United States. She
finishes tenth in a field of 12 at Hialeah.

Barbara Jo Rubin becomes the first woman jockey
to enter the winner's circle, riding Cohesion to a win
at Charles Town, West Virginia, and Bravy Galaxy (a
13-to-1 shot) to a title at Aqueduct.

The Lady Godiva Handicap at Suffolk Downs in Boston
features an all-female field of jockeys, including Barbara Ader, Diane Crump, Penny Ann Early, Connie
Hendricks, Robyn Smith, Brenda Wilson, and Tuesdee
Testa.

Janet Lynn wins the national figure skating championship.

Waterskier Stephanie Stephens Shackelford wins the American Water Ski Association Western Regional Overall women's title once again. She takes first place in the slalom event in both the Tournament of Champions and the Masters American Water Ski Association Tournament.

1970   The CIAW and the DGWS add badminton, swimming and diving, and volleyball to the list of sports in which they sponsor national intercollegiate championships for American women.

Heidi O'Rourke wins AAU medals in the indoor and outdoor solo, the indoor and outdoor duet, and the indoor team synchronized swimming competitions. She is named to the all-American synchronized swimming team for the second consecutive year.

Swimming Hall of Fame inductees include Florence Chadwick, Olga Dorfner, and Claire Galligan.

Nancy Myrick wins the U.S. Nationals in archery for the second time in her career.

Hortense Wood Hardesty is the second woman in ATA history to be handicapped at the 17-yard line in trapshooting.

Margaret Murdock betters top riflemen at the world championship competition.

Cathy Rigby wins a silver medal in the balance beam competition at the World Gymnastics Championships, becoming the first American gymnast to accomplish that feat.

Donna Caponi wins her second consecutive U.S. Women's Open golf championship.

Kathy Whitworth leads women golfers in tournament wins for the sixth consecutive year.

Dorothy Fothergill wins the first of her 6 WIBC crowns.

Joanne Chapman is a member of the Iowa State championship bowling team for the second time in her career. She also wins the WIBC all-events title.

Doris Coburn captains the WIBC championship team.

Helen Duval and Catherine Fellmeth are elected to the WIBC Hall of Fame.

Winifred Berger is voted WIBC member emeritus.

Marian E. Washington begins a 3-year basketball career with the Baytown Piperettes.

Jean Daves sets records for most wins in a season (40) and most innings pitched (340).

Dorothy Wilkinson is elected to the National Softball Hall of Fame.

Diane Crump is the first female jockey to race in the Kentucky Derby.

Janet Lynn wins her second straight national figure skating championship.

Betsy Clifford is a gold medalist in the world championship skiing competition, winning the giant slalom.

Seventeen-year-old Sally Younger sets a waterskiing speed record of 105.14 miles per hour.

1971   The CIAW is reorganized on a regional basis and becomes the Association for Intercollegiate Athletics for Women (AIAW).

Florence Chambers Newkirk is inducted into the San Diego Hall of Champions. In her swimming career, she has collected more than 300 medals and 136 trophies. She is the founder and director of the Florence Chambers Swim Club, where she has helped to develop many top swimmers, Florence Chadwick among them.

Lynn Colella wins 2 gold medals (200-meter breaststroke

and butterfly) and a bronze (100-meter breaststroke) at the Pan American Games.

Sandy Nielson of the U.S. takes the gold in the 100-meter freestyle.

Heidi O'Rourke wins 3 gold medals in synchronized swimming at the Pan American Games. She also wins 6 AAU titles, and is named to the all-American synchronized swimming team for the third year in a row.

Punkin Flock wins another singles title in trapshooting.

Karen Hantze Susman is inducted into the San Diego Hall of Champions.

Billie Jean King wins the U.S. Open women's singles title.

Marita Redondo is the U.S. women's amateur tennis champion. She also takes the girls' national singles and doubles titles.

Iris Davis of Pompano Beach, Florida, sets an American women's record with a time of 10.2 seconds in the 100-yard dash. She wins the 100-meter dash in the Pan American Games and is a member of the gold-medal-winning 400-meter relay team.

Patty Jean Johnson wins a gold medal at the Pan American Games for her performance in the 100-meter hurdles.

Joan Moore Rice ties for first place in the Elite Nationals gymnastics competition.

At 16, Laura Baugh becomes the youngest player to win the U.S. Women's Amateur Golf Championship.

JoAnne Carner is the U.S. Women's Open golf champion.

Ruth Jensen wins the $60,000 Sears Women's World Classic, the richest event on the women's professional golf tour.

Georgene Cordes of Bloomington, Minnesota, sets a

record for 18 consecutive strikes bowled in sanctioned play.

At age 19, Lorie Nichols is the youngest to win an all-events title in bowling.

Barbara Duns wins the women's national intercollegiate all-events bowling title.

Joanne Chapman wins the IWBA singles title.

Shirley Garms and Tess Morris Small are elected to the WIBC Hall of Fame.

Marian E. Washington receives an honorable mention in elections for the AAU All-American basketball team.

Virginia Busick is elected to the National Softball Hall of Fame.

Clara Teyssier wins the Intermediate California State Road Cycling Championship.

Mary Bacon is the first woman jockey to ride 100 winners.

Cheryl White, riding her father's horse, Jetolara, at Waterford Park in Chester, West Virginia, becomes the first black woman jockey in American thoroughbred history to win a race.

Janet Lynn wins the U.S. national figure skating championship for the third consecutive year.

Suzy Chaffee is the first woman to enter a freestyle skiing competition.

Joyce Hoffman Lancour is the U.S. women's surfing champion.

IV. THE TITLE IX ERA
1972–1987

> No person in the United States shall, on the basis
> of sex, be excluded from participation in, be de-
> nied the benefits of, or be subjected to discrimi-
> nation under any education program or activity
> receiving Federal financial assistance.
>
> --Public Law 92-318

1972   Title IX of the Education Amendments of 1972 (P.L.
       92-318) is passed by the U.S. Congress.

       In response to a national invitation, 73 colleges become
       associate members and 205 colleges and universities
       become charter members of the newly formed AIAW.

       Melissa Belote of Silver Spring, Maryland, wins 3
       gold medals in Olympic swimming events at Munich--
       the 100- and 200-meter backstroke and the 4 × 100
       medley relay.

       With a time of 1 minute, 13.58 seconds, Cathy Carr
       wins the 100-meter breaststroke competition at the
       Olympic Games.

       Sandy Nielson wins the first place title in the 100-
       meter freestyle.

       Karen Moe wins a gold medal in the 200-meter butter-
       fly.

       Keena Rothhammer of the U.S. takes the gold in the
       800-meter freestyle.

       Micki King wins the Olympic gold in the 3-meter spring-
       board diving competition.

Gail Johnson wins synchronized swimming titles in the duet and team competitions at the Canadian Nationals and in the solo, duet, and team competitions at the Tri-Country meet.

Heidi O'Rourke is elected to the Helms Synchronized Swimming Hall of Fame.

Punkin Flock shoots 199 out of 200 in the Florida State Trapshooting Championships, besting all other entrants, both men and women.

ATA Hall of Fame inductees include Hortense Wood Hardesty, Iva Pembridge Jarvis, Dorothy Marker, Frances King Garlington, Mary Meadows, and Punkin Flock.

Billie Jean King wins her fourth Wimbledon singles crown.

Women tennis pros receive prize money equal to that of the men at the U.S. Open Tournament.

Marita Redondo is the U.S. amateur women's tennis champion.

Susan Hagey, winner of the national girls' 14-and-under hardcourt singles and doubles, is a member of the team from San Diego that wins the national junior girls' city team championship at Kansas City.

Marian E. Washington is the Missouri Valley AAU and National Junior Olympic discus champion. In addition, she is named to the AAU All-American basketball team.

Wyomia Tyus wins her third Olympic gold medal in track. Kathy Hammond of Sacramento, California, sets an American record in the 400-meter run and wins the bronze medal in Olympic competition.

Iris Davis takes fourth place in the 100-meter dash.

Madeline Jackson-Manning runs the second leg of the 1600-meter relay. The American team takes a silver medal.

Olga Connolly competes in her fourth Olympic discus competition as an American.

Kathy Schmidt of Long Beach, California, wins the bronze medal in Olympic javelin competition.

Nina Kuscsik is the first of 9 females to cross the finish line in the Boston Marathon. She finishes ahead of 800 male runners.

Cathy Rigby leads the American gymnastics team to Munich for the XXth Olympiad, but wins no Olympic medals.

Joan Moore Rice ties for first place in the Elite National gymnastics competition for the second consecutive year. She ranks a respectable 21st in Olympic gymnastics competition.

Jean Balukas of Brooklyn, New York, wins her first U.S. Open pocket billiards championship at the age of 14. Her prize is $1,500.

Kathy Whitworth is the LPGA leading money winner once again. The LPGA awards its first tournament prize purse in excess of $100,000.

Susie Maxwell Berning wins the U.S. Women's Open golf tournament.

Golfer Carol Mann holds a clinic for 150 girls. With the enactment of Title IX, more girls and women will have opportunities to participate in sports.

D. D. Jacobson wins the WIBC singles tournament with a record series of 737.

Dorothy Fothergill wins her first WIBC Queens title.

Doris Coburn captains the WIBC championship team for the second time in her career. The team compiles the third highest total score in the history of the tournament.

Stella Hartrick and Beverly Ortner are elected to the WIBC Hall of Fame.

Ann Rand is inducted into the IWBA Hall of Fame.

The New York State Court of Appeals upholds the
right of Bernice Gera to be an umpire in professional
baseball.

Bertha Tickey is named to the National Softball Hall
of Fame.

Clara Teyssier wins the 3,000 women's national pursuit
title and the California state pursuit and road championships. She sets two American cycling records at the
Italian Swiss Colony Road Race held in Asti, California.

Dianne Holum is the 1500-meter women's Olympic speed
skating champion.

Anne Henning wins the 500-meter Olympic speed skating
title.

Janet Lynn wins her fourth consecutive national championship in figure skating.

Barbara Cochran takes the Olympic gold in the women's
slalom competition.

1973 The AIAW's membership list now includes 405 institutions.

The National Association for Girls and Women in Sport
(NAGWS), formerly the DGWS, finally permits the
granting of financial aid to American women athletes
in colleges and universities.

At the University of Miami in Coral Gables, Florida,
golfer Terry Williams is the first woman to receive
a full-tuition athletic scholarship.

The Women's Equity Action League demands that the
Department of Health, Education, and Welfare ensure
that schools grant students of both sexes equal access
to sports and coaching facilities.

The Pennsylvania Justice Department rules that women
may be licensed to box and wrestle in Pennsylvania.

Julie Ludovina, a 127-pound 16-year-old, competes
in her first interscholastic wrestling match, thus becoming the first female high school wrestler in California.

Swimmer Shirley Babashoff wins gold medals in the
200- and 400-meter freestyle races at the World Championship Games. She also wins 2 silver medals in
relay competition.

Melissa Belote wins a gold and 2 silver medals in swimming at the World Championships at Belgrade.

Keena Rothhammer wins the 200-meter freestyle swimming event at the World Championship Games.

Gail Johnson wins gold medals in the duet and team
synchronized swimming competitions at Belgrade.

Nikki Franke is a member of the World University
Games fencing team for the first of 4 years.

Vonda Kemmerer places second at the Championship
of the Americas Field Tournament in archery.

Joanne Stawske wins the women's national high-power
rifle championship.

Black Sports magazine announces the first 38 members
of the Black Sports Hall of Fame; among them are
Althea Gibson (tennis) and Wilma Rudolph (track).

Chris Evert takes the women's singles title at the
U.S. Clay Court Tennis Championships in Indianapolis.

Billie Jean King wins her fifth Wimbledon singles crown.
In a $100,000 winner-take-all tennis match at the Hous-
ton Astrodome, she beats Bobby Riggs before 30,492
people, the largest audience in tennis history.

Susan Hagey wins the singles competition in the national girls' 16-and-under hardcourt tournament.

Marian E. Washington wins the Missouri Valley AAU

and the U.S. Track and Field Finals championships in
the discus throw. She sets a USTFF distance record.

Fran Sichting sets a new American record, running
220 yards in 23.2 seconds.

Kathy Schmidt sets a new American record in the
javelin throw: 208 feet, 1 inch.

Joan Moore Rice takes first place in the Elite National
gymnastics competition.

Laura Baugh is declared the LPGA Rookie of the Year
by Golf Digest.

Susie Maxwell Berning wins the U.S. Women's Open
golf tournament for the second year in a row.

Kathy Whitworth is the LPGA leading money winner
for the eighth year.

Barbara Duns and her teammates from San Diego State
University win the national intercollegiate bowling
title.

Mildred Martorella wins the U.S. Women's Open Bowling
Tournament and is the first to roll a perfect game in a
PWBA tournament.

Dorothy Fothergill wins her second WIBC Queens title.

Joanne Chapman is a member of the WIBC championship
team for the second time in her career.

Connie Powers is elected to the WIBC Hall of Fame.

Leta Smith is inducted into the IWBA Hall of Fame.

The U.S. Volleyball Association (USVBA) honors Patty
Dowdell as Rookie of the Year.

New Jersey becomes the first state in the country
to allow girls to play on Little League baseball teams.
Little League managers in Ypsilanti, Michigan, however,
refuse to allow Carolyn King to play baseball.

Marilyn Rau is named an all-American softball player
for the first of 9 times in a single decade.

Bertha Tickey is inducted into the Connecticut Hall
of Fame.

Electees to the National Softball Hall of Fame include
Estelle Caito and Gloria May.

Eleven-year-old Becky Gorton sets out from Olympia,
Washington, and bicycles to Boston, Massachusetts,
arriving 46 days later.

Christy Fletcher wins 5 blue ribbons to become the
champion junior equestrienne of California.

Robyn Smith wins the Paumonok Handicap at Aqueduct,
becoming the first woman to top the field in a stakes
race.

Janet Lynn wins the national figure skating championship for the fifth consecutive year.

1974   The Women's Sports Foundation is established.

Dr. Nell C. Jackson is inducted into the Tuskegee
Institute Hall of Fame.

The American Alliance for Health, Physical Education,
and Recreation (AAHPER) presents its Distinguished
Service Award to Dr. Donnis Thompson.

Sandra Keshka swims the English Channel from France
to England in 10 hours, 30 minutes. Her skills earn
her a place on the men's varsity swim team at San
Diego State University.

Shirley Babashoff sets world records in the 200- and
400-meter freestyle swimming events and is named
Sportswoman of the Year.

Gail Johnson wins the solo, duet, and team competitions
in synchronized swimming at the Japanese championships.
She is the first synchronized swimmer to win the Sullivan
Award.

Lucille Lessard wins the world field archery championship.

Susan Natrass wins the world championship of trapshooting.

Mary Feeney is the only female member of the U.S. Navy rifle team. She wins the women's high-power rifle championships at Camp Perry, Ohio.

Chris Evert wins her first singles title at Wimbledon.

Billie Jean King wins the U.S. Open women's singles title.

Cathy Williams wins the first women's professional racquetball tournament.

Ten years after her first Olympic victory, Wyomia Tyus completes an undefeated track season.

Joan Moore Rice takes another first place at the Elite National gymnastics competition, thus qualifying as the best amateur gymnast in the United States.

JoAnne Carner leads LPGA money winners with total earnings of $87,094 for the year.

Joan Taylor of Syracuse, New York, bowls 27 spares in a row.

Doris Coburn is the third woman to bowl an 800 series.

Judy Soutar wins the WIBC team, all-events, and Queens titles.

Joan Holm is a member of the victorious bowling team from the United States at the American Zone Tournament in Caracas, Venezuela.

Olga Gloor wins the all-events title at the American Zone competition.

Floy Harmsen is named IWBA life member.

Joanne Chapman is inducted into the IWBA Hall of
Fame.

Merle Matthews and Joan Holm are elected to the WIBC
Hall of Fame.

Marian E. Washington is named to the AAU All-American
basketball team for the second time.   She also competes
in team handball at the Canadian Games, and accepts
a position as director of women's intercollegiate athletics
and head basketball coach at the University of Kansas.

Little League officials at the national level announce
that girls are allowed to play baseball.

Shirley Topley leads the Pacific Coast Women's Softball
League in hitting for the second time in her career.

Julie Batchelor and her husband conquer the Congo
River in a canoe.   They travel 2,600 miles in 128
days.

One year after turning professional, Janet Lynn wins
her first professional figure skating championship.

Dorothy Hamill wins her first U.S. figure skating
championship.

Betsy Clifford is the silver medalist in downhill skiing
at the world championships.

1975   A law allowing girls to practice and compete in all
interscholastic sports, including football and wrestling,
is upheld by the Pennsylvania Commonwealth Court.
The court also declares that a Pennsylvania Interscholastic Athletic Association bylaw banning girls
from competing with boys is unconstitutional.

Dr. Doris Corbett receives the Distinguished Faculty
Award from the Department of Physical Education and
Recreation at Howard University in Washington, D.C.
She also receives the Outstanding Service Award for
leadership to physical education from the undergraduate
majors' club.

Anne Herman, who is paralyzed, wins a gold medal in the backstroke and silver medals in the freestyle and the breaststroke at the Pan American Games for the Disabled in Mexico City.

Shirley Babashoff wins a bronze, 2 silver, and 2 gold medals at the world championship swimming competition.

Gail Johnson continues her winning ways in synchronized swimming, taking the solo and team titles at Cali, Colombia.

Nikki Franke is a member of the American fencing team, winning silver and bronze medals at the Pan American Games. She is the National Women's Foil Champion this year.

Billie Jean King wins her sixth Wimbledon singles crown.

Chris Evert wins the U.S. Open women's tennis title for the first of 4 consecutive years.

Evelyn Boldrick Howard is elected to the San Diego Hall of Champions for her accomplishments in badminton.

Wyomia Tyus records her second undefeated track season.

Madeline Jackson-Manning is inducted into the U.S. Track and Field Hall of Fame.

Amy Alcott is named Rookie of the Year on the women's professional golf tour.

Dottie Morgan of the U.S. Navy wins the all-events title at the Interservice Bowling Championships. She and partner Carol Gunder take the doubles title.

Cathy Townsend is the World Cup bowling champion.

Doris Coburn wins the Red Crown Classic, the richest women's bowling tournament, and bowls a perfect game.

Judy Soutar is named BWAA Bowler of the Year.

Dorothea Fort is a charter inductee in the Waterloo Metro WBA Hall of Fame.

Cecelia Winandy and Mildred Martorella are elected to the WIBC Hall of Fame.

Laura Albrecht is elected an IWBA life member.

Vera Schlenker is inducted into the IWBA Hall of Fame.

Volleyball great Mary Jo Peppler wins the first Women's Superstar competition.

The American media present the first televised women's collegiate basketball game.

Lusia Harris-Stewart is a member of the AIAW National Basketball Championship team. She is named a Kodak All-American for the first of 3 seasons.

Marian E. Washington tours the U.S.S.R. as a member of the American women's basketball team. She also represents the U.S. in team handball at the World Games.

Marjorie Law and Kathryn King are elected to the National Softball Hall of Fame.

Ann Turbyne raises 410 pounds in a 2-handed dead lift at Winslow, Maine.

Lynn Silliman is coxswain for the American women's crew team that takes a silver medal in world championship competition in London.

Karen Stead becomes the first girl to win the world championship in gravity racing at the All-American Soap Box Derby.

Dorothy Hamill wins her second consecutive national figure skating title.

1976 Olga Connolly, appearing in her fifth Olympics as an

American, is the first woman to carry the Stars and
Stripes in the opening ceremonies.

Tina Sloan Green is appointed chairperson of the Committee on the Status of Minority Women within the
AIAW.

Dr. Donnis Thompson is named Female Educator of
the Year by the University of Northern Colorado Alum-
ni Association. The Hawaii State Legislature adopts
a resolution commending her for developing the women's
athletic program at the University of Hawaii.

Dr. Evie G. Dennis is named women's manager of the
U.S. Olympic track and field team. She also begins
to serve as national chair for Women's Track and Field,
member of the U.S. Olympic Committee Board of Directors, first vice-president of the Rocky Mountain Association of the AAU, and member of the Executive Committee of the AAU.

Shirley Babashoff sets 3 American records in preliminary
competition and 3 more in the finals. She sets a world
record in the 800-meter freestyle at the Olympic Games,
where she wins a gold and 4 silver medals. Swimming
World Magazine names her American Swimmer of the
Year.

Jennifer Chandler takes the 3-meter springboard diving
title at the Senior AAU Championships and goes on to
win a gold medal at the XXIst Olympiad in Montreal.
The youngest diver to win an Olympic gold medal, she
compiles the highest total score in Olympic diving
history.

Sylvia Fortier is recognized as the world champion
of synchronized swimming.

Luann Ryon wins her first Olympic gold medal in archery.

Kathleen Roberts wins the Oklahoma State Women's
Archery Championship.

Carol Pelosi wins the women's crossbow competition at
the National Archery Association Target Championships.

Ila Hill becomes the international skeet shooting champion at the U.S. International Skeet and Clay Pigeon
contest.

Margaret Murdock wins the silver medal in Olympic
rifle competition.

Mary Stidworthy wins the NRA Championship in the
standard rifle prone position.

Nancy Clark wins the National Rifle and Pistol Championship in the women's high-powered rifle category
at Camp Perry, Ohio.

Sherri Lewellen wins the women's title in the small-
bore position at the National Rifle and Pistol Championships.

Cheryl Stearns takes first place in the National Parachute Jumping Championships.

Chris Evert wins her second Wimbledon singles title
and the singles title at the U.S. Open as well.

Wendy Chase and Linda Wolfe claim the National Women's
Platform Tennis Doubles Championship in Summit, New
Jersey.

Gretchen Spruance wins the squash racquets competition
at the U.S. championships in Philadelphia.

Cathy Williams and Sue Carow win the racquetball
doubles championship in Houston, Texas.

Madeline Jackson-Manning runs 800 meters in under
2 minutes at the Olympic Games.

Jan Merrill runs 3 miles in 16 minutes, 37 seconds,
taking first place at the AAU Women's Cross Country
Championships.

Wyomia Tyus is elected to the Track and Field Hall
of Fame.

Roxanne Pierce wins the All-Around Gymnast Award at

the National Senior Athletic Union Championships in
Philadelphia.

Pam Harrington wins the U.S. Gymnastics Federation
Championship.

Shelly Grant places first in the women's open trampo-
line competition in Ohio.

Jean Balukas of Brooklyn wins $1,700 in the Women's
U.S. Open Pocket Billiards Championships. The men's
winner collects $4,500.

Diane Kopicki wins 22 games and loses 4 to become
the National Girls' Champion in marbles.

Black belt Denise DeHaven is ranked first in the U.S.
Karate Association Grand Nationals.

Margaret Castro and Maureen Braziel win the Women's
Open International Judo Competition in East Lansing,
Michigan.

JoAnne Carner wins her second U.S. Women's Open
golf championship.

Judy Rankin is awarded $32,000 in the Colgate-Dinah
Shore Golf Tournament. She becomes the first LPGA
money winner to top $100,000 in earnings for a single
year.

Amy Alcott wins $15,000 in the Colgate Far East Open
Golf Tournament with a 3-round score of 211.

Donna Caponi Young wins $35,000 with a 4-round
score of 282 at the Carlton Golf Tournament in California.

Kaye Minions claims the lawn bowling singles title in
the National Open Tournament at Clearwater, Florida.

Mary Eldridge wins the Women's National Winter Shuf-
fleboard Championship at St. Petersburg, Florida.

Doris Shortt places first in the National Duckpin Bowling Tournament, knocking down 467 pins.

Betty Morris pins down the Brunswick Red Crown
World Invitational Bowling Championship with a season
average of 204.9.

Cathy Townsend takes first place in the Bowling Tournament of the Americas.

Lo Borschuk receives the 25-year participation award
from the WIBC.

WIBC Hall of Fame electees include Doris Coburn,
Elvira Toepfer, Winifred Berger, Judy Soutar, and
Olga Gloor.

Nellie Nicholson is inducted into the IWBA Hall of
Fame.

Dorothy Haas receives the Distinguished Service Award
from the Metropolitan New York Bowling Writers' Association.

Marian E. Washington is a member of the U.S. Women's
Olympic handball team.

The U.S. Field Hockey Association becomes the only
Olympic governing body to exclude men.

Darlene Bailey is voted Most Valuable Player after
leading her volleyball team (Nick's Fish Market) to an
AAU championship.

Lusia Harris-Stewart, a member of the silver medal
Olympic basketball team, is named Mississippi's Best
Amateur Athlete of the Year.

Ann Meyers, also a member of the American silver-
medal-winning basketball team, is named an all-American
for the fourth time.

Joan Joyce, whose fastball has been clocked at 118
miles per hour, leads the Connecticut Falcons to a
World Series win in the International Women's Professional Softball Association.

Barbara Reinalda bats .450 and is voted Most Valuable

Player on the ASA All-American women's team. She
also wins the Bertha Tickey Award.

Alberta Kohls Sims, Pat Walker, and Pat Harrison are
elected to the National Softball Hall of Fame.

The first Olympic crew competition for women takes
place. Lynn Silliman is the coxswain for the American
women's 8-oared crew. Her boat wins the bronze
medal.

Cindy Todd finishes first in the Masters Water Skiing
Tournament at Callaway Gardens, Georgia.

Lynn Boyer wins the Women's International Surfing
Championship.

Paula Murphy drives 26,412.21 miles in the U.S. Global
Record Run in 105 days.

Janet Guthrie enters the World 600, becoming the
first woman to drive in a major stock-car race.

Kitty O'Neill, strapped into a 48,000-horsepower rocket
car, reaches a speed of 512.71 miles per hour.

Connie Combs wins the women's world barrel racing
title at the National Rodeo Finals in Oklahoma City
and becomes the world champion.

Sheila Young averages 27.49 miles per hour on speed
skates to set a 500-meter record. She wins a gold
medal at the Innsbruck Winter Olympics.

Nineteen-year-old Dorothy Hamill wins the U.S. Na-
tional Figure Skating Championship in Colorado Springs.
She also captures the triple crown at the World Figure
Skating Championships in Gothenburg, Sweden.

Lori Benton takes the bronze medal at the U.S. National Figure Skating Championship.

Natalie Dunn outclasses the field in women's figure
roller skating at the World Artistic Championships in
Rome.

Roxanne Steinke wins both women's racing titles at the World Championship Snowmobiling Derby in Eagle River, Wisconsin.

Barb Yearley and Judy Rinaldi win the Women's World Series of Snowmobiling at St. Paul, Minnesota.

Deborah Molburg takes first place in the Canadian International Sled Dog Derby, steering her dog team along a 67.5-mile trail.

1977   The AIAW sponsors 20 national championships in 12 different sports for American collegiate women athletes.

Dr. Nell C. Jackson becomes a member of the Black Athlete Hall of Fame.

Melissa Belote captures women's national collegiate titles in the 100- and 200-yard backstroke and the 400-yard individual medley.   She is named the Outstanding Female College Swimmer by the AIAW and Broderick Award Committees.

Cynthia Potter McInguale executes 3 1/2 somersaults from a 3-meter board.

April Moon shoots an arrow 810 yards, 1 foot, 9 inches for a world record.

Susan Natrass wins the world championship of trapshooting.

Pam Shelby wins the women's doubles and overall titles at the Grand American trapshooting championships.

Fourteen-year-old Tracy Austin (only 5 feet tall and weighing 93 pounds) beats fourth-seeded Sue Barker in a mere 59 minutes in their U.S. Open tennis match at Forest Hills.   She wins her first tennis tournament--the Avon Futures--and is the youngest competitor in Wimbledon history.   By the end of the year, she is the fourth-ranked tennis player in the world.

The court upholds Renee Richards' request to compete

as a female in the U.S. Open, stating that her age (43) counterbalances her advantages as a 6'2" former male athlete.

Chris Evert wins her third consecutive U.S. Open women's singles title.

The All-England Tennis Club at Wimbledon agrees to employ 10 girls, along with the usual 70 boys, to retrieve balls at its annual tournament.

Lynn Winbigler throws the discus 187 feet, 2 inches for a U.S. women's record.

Kathy Schmidt sets a world record for the javelin throw: 227 feet, 5 inches.

Hollis Stacy takes first place in the U.S. Women's Open golf tournament.

Judy Rankin is the LPGA leading money winner for the second consecutive year.

Mae Bolt and her Allgauer's Fireside Restaurant team win their fourth WIBC championship.

Electees to the WIBC Hall of Fame include Dorothy Haas, Helen Shablis, LaVerne Carter, Nine Van Camp Burns, and Helen Baetz.

Basketball player Lusia Harris-Stewart is the winner of the first Broderick Cup.   Named for Tom Broderick, president of the Thomas Broderick Company, the award is given to the nation's outstanding woman athlete.

On January 4, Mary Shane becomes major league baseball's first woman television announcer.   She is hired by the Chicago White Sox to handle the play-by-play commentary.

Michelle Thomas pitches the Northern Iowa softball team to a college title.

Nedra Jerry sets the UCLA career home run record.

Cheryl Kay Kempf pitches for the ASA championship team.

Kim Miller is named to the first All-Conference softball team for the first of 3 seasons.

Venus Jennings is named Colorado Sports Woman for her softball accomplishments.

Anita L. DeFrantz wins the national championship in straight pairs rowing competition.

Betty Cook, the only woman competitor, wins the World Off Shore Racing title in powerboating.

Shirley "Cha Cha" Muldowney records a velocity of 252.1 miles per hour in her dragster.

Janet Guthrie is the first woman to compete in the Indianapolis 500.

Linda Fratianne wins the U.S. and world figure skating championships.

Lisa Marie Allen takes second place in the national championships.

Sharon Crawford of New England is the U.S. orienteering champion.

1978   The AIAW's membership list expands to include 827 colleges and universities.

Seventy-three percent of the respondents to a membership survey of the NAGWS support the concept of a legal identity for the AIAW that would be separate from the NAGWS.

A judicial decision allows female sportswriters equal access to the locker rooms of male athletes.

Dr. Nell C. Jackson receives a presidential citation from the NAGWS.

Dr. Doris Corbett receives the Appreciation Award
from the AAHPER in Washington, D.C.

Tracy Caulkins is named the James E. Sullivan Memorial
Trophy winner for her accomplishments and sportsmanship in swimming.

Penny Dean sets a new world record for swimming
the English Channel: 7 hours, 40 minutes.

Linda Jezek is the world champion in the 100-meter
backstroke.

Mary-Joan Pennington wins the world championship in
the 100-meter butterfly.

Nikki Franke captains the championship women's foil
team.   She is also a member of the national fencing
team, and competes in the world championships.

At 18, Judi Adams wins the Championship of the Americas archery competition.

Jacqueline Smith scores 10 consecutive "dead centers"
in world parachute jumping.

A team of American women reach the summit of Anna-
purna in Nepal.

Chris Evert wins her fourth consecutive U.S. Open
women's singles tennis title, defeating 16-year-old
Pam Shriver in the finals.

Billie Jean King and Martina Navratilova team up to
win the U.S. Open women's doubles title.

Martina Navratilova also wins the women's singles title
at Wimbledon.

Cheryl Carton of San Diego, California, wins her first
national badminton championship.

The first International All-Women's Marathon is held.

Jane Frederick sets a world record for the heptathlon.

Hollis Stacy wins her second consecutive U.S. Women's Open golf tournament championship.

Nancy Lopez is the leading money winner in the LPGA, with a total of $189,813.

Mae Bolt wins the WIBC singles championship and is elected to the Hall of Fame.

Dorothea Fort receives the WIBC 25-year participation award.

Gertrude Frohwein is inducted into the IWBA Hall of Fame.

Pat Dryer and Theresa Kelone are elected to the WIBC Hall of Fame.

New members of the U.S. women's national volleyball team include Carolyn Becker, Laurie Flachmeier, Rita Crockett, Debbi Green, and Sue Woodstra.

Rita Crockett is named Rookie of the Year by the U.S. Volleyball Association and Most Valuable Player from the South All-Star team.

Rose Magers is named Most Valuable Player on the volleyball team at the University of Houston. Sherryl Moore shares the award.

In the debut of the Women's Professional Basketball League, Debra Waddy-Rossow scores 30 points for the Chicago Hustle, as they defeat the Milwaukee Does, 92-87.

Jill Larson is an All-Big Eight softball selection for the first of 3 seasons.

Suzie Gaw is a member of the ASA All-American first team.

Norma Eschenbrenner Ante is elected to the National Softball Hall of Fame.

Anita L. DeFrantz is the national champion in straight

pairs rowing competition for the second year in a
row.

Lynn McKenzie is named National Finals Rodeo (NFR)
Rookie of the Year and is awarded the title of World
Champion Barrel Racer.

Linda Fratianne takes her second consecutive U.S.
figure skating title.

Cathy "Cat" Davis becomes the first woman to receive
a license to box professionally in New York State.

New Englander Sharon Crawford wins the U.S. orienteering championship.

1979   Dr. Alpha Vernell Alexander, instructor of athletic
administration at Temple University, is named "one of
the 79 people to watch in 1979" by Philadelphia Magazine.

Dr. Donnis Thompson is the administrator for the
World University Games in Mexico City. She also
begins a 2-year career of service as a member of the
board of directors of the U.S. Collegiate Sports Council.

Dr. Evie G. Dennis is the chief administrator for female athletes at the Pan American Games. She is
also chief of the delegation for the U.S. track and
field team at the World Cup competition. She serves
as vice-president of the AAU, and receives the Distinguished Service Award from the Denver Regional
Council of Government.

C. Vivian Stringer of Cheyney State College is named
Coach of the Year by the Philadelphia sportswriters.

Sabrina Jackintell soars 12,557.75 meters in a glider
for a world record.

Diana Nyad is the first person to swim from the Ba-
hamas to Florida.

Kim Linehan sets a world record in the 1500-meter
freestyle swim.

Nikki Franke is a member of the American fencing
team at the Pan American Games and wins 2 medals
in the competition. She is inducted into the Brooklyn
College Hall of Fame.

Judi Adams places second at the World Target Archery
Tournament.

Pam Shelby wins her second women's doubles and overall titles at the Grand American trapshooting championships.

Betty Ann Foxworth becomes editor emeritus and field
editor for Trap and Field. She also collaborates with
trapshooting historian Jimmy Robinson on a book en-
titled All American Trapshooting Teams.

Martina Navratilova wins her second women's singles
title at Wimbledon.

Tracy Austin wins the U.S. Open tennis singles championship.

Chris Evert Lloyd wins the singles title at the French
Open.

Sprinter Evelyn Ashford is the first American since
1968 to break East Germany's domination of the 100-
and 200-meter races. She wins both races at the
World Cup Championships and is voted Woman Athlete
of the Year.

Nancy Lopez is the LPGA's leading money winner for
the second consecutive year.

Billie Jean Lee wins the Classic Division singles championship in the California Women's Bowling Association
tournament. She is elected to the CWBA Hall of Fame.

Nellie Nicholson is named member emeritus of the IWBA.

Lo Borschuk is inducted into the IWBA Hall of Fame.

WIBC Hall of Fame electees include Ethel Sablatnik,
Anita Cantaline, Gertrude Dornblasser, Phyllis Notaro,
Catherine Menne, Ellen Kelly, Mabel Marrs, Martha
Hoffman, and Val Mikiel.

Denise Corlett is selected UCLA's Athlete of the Year
for her accomplishments on the volleyball court.

Debbi Green and Julie Vollersten play for the U.S.
women's national volleyball team.

Several students from San Diego State University play
on the team that wins the AAU volleyball championship.

Chris Prieboy is named AIAW All-State Most Valuable
Player in basketball and receives an invitation to the
Olympic trials.

Ann Meyers becomes the first woman to join the National Basketball Association when she signs a contract
with the Indiana Pacers.

Doris Goodwin becomes the first woman reporter to
enter a baseball clubhouse as the Boston Red Sox
open their doors to all media personnel.

Rhonda Clark pitches the Oklahoma City Jets to an
ASA 18-and-under title.

Kathy Van Wyk and Shirley "Missy" Mapes play softball for the national champion Texas Women's University team. Van Wyk is named Texas AIAW Player of
the Year. Mapes becomes a member of the Pan American softball team, along with Marilyn Rau, Barbara
Reinalda, Dot Richardson, and Suzie Gaw.

Gretchen Larson, Kathy Van Wyk, and Suzie Gaw
are named to the ASA All-American second team.

Michelle Thomas pitches a perfect game in national
softball competition.

Donna Wolfe is elected to the National Softball Hall
of Fame.

Karen Roberge wins the women's overall open division
title at the National Water Ski Championships. She
also wins the Masters' International Cup.

Lynn McKenzie and her horse do well in NFR competition, earning second place in the world championships.

Beth Heiden is the world speed skating champion.

Linda Fratianne wins both the U.S. and the world
figure skating championships.

Sharon Crawford wins her third consecutive U.S.
orienteering championship.

1980 The Women's Sports Hall of Fame holds its inauguration.

Dr. Alpha Vernell Alexander, assistant women's athletic
director at Temple University, is the youngest black
woman in the United States to hold an administrative
position like this at a large university.

Dr. Doris Corbett is listed in the World's Who's Who
of Women. She serves as NAGWS President.

Dr. Evie G. Dennis is again named the women's manager
of the U.S. Olympic track and field team. She begins
4 years of service as vice-president of the U.S. Olympic
Committee (USOC).

A 35-cent U.S. stamp is issued in honor of Blanche
Stuart Scott (1886-1970), the first woman to fly solo.

The first Women's Judo Championships are held in
Madison Square Garden, New York.

Tina Sloan Green becomes president of the Women's
Lacrosse Association at Philadelphia College and is
the founder of the Philadelphia Inner City Field Hockey
Program.

C. Vivian Stringer is nominated Coach of the Year by
the Pennsylvania Association for Intercollegiate Athletics
for Women for her success in basketball.

Kris Unsicker, disabled in an automobile accident,
wins a gold medal in archery at the Olympiad for the
Physically Disabled in Arnhem, Holland. She wins
the woman's pentathlon (which includes archery, swimming, shot-put, javelin, and 100-meter dash competition)
at the National Wheelchair Games.

Cindy Vezzetti is an all-American in archery for the
first of 3 consecutive years.

Laura Cale wins top honors at the U.S. Indoor Archery
competition.

Ruth Caillouet is the Southern Collegiate Champion
and the Louisiana State Indoor and Outdoor Champion
in archery.

Donna Gelnett is Collegiate Archery Champion for
the first of 2 years.

Judi Adams is the U.S. National Champion in archery.
She is selected for the Olympic team, but cannot compete due to the American boycott of the Summer Games
in Moscow.

The American boycott keeps many other talented Ameri-
can women out of competition in the XXIInd Olympiad.
Among them are volleyball players Rita Crockett, Debbi
Green, and Julie Vollersten; canoer and kayaker Leslie
Klein; number-one-ranked fencer Nikki Franke; runner
Madeline Jackson-Manning, and field hockey players
Beth Beglin and Sheryl Johnson.

Chris Evert Lloyd wins another U.S. Open women's
singles tennis championship and her second consecutive French Open title.

Billie Jean King and Martina Navratilova win the U.S.
Open doubles tennis title once again.

Tracy and John Austin become the first brother-sister
team in history to win the mixed doubles title at Wimbledon. Tracy is ranked number one in the world.

Cheryl Carton wins the women's national badminton title.

TRACY AUSTIN (tennis)

SENDA BERENSON (basketball)
(Courtesy of Smith College Archives)

Above: MAUREEN CONNOLLY BRINKER (tennis)
             (Courtesy of San Diego Hall of Champions)
Below: VALERIE BRISCO-HOOKS (track)
             (Courtesy of UPI/Bettmann Newsphotos)

Above: FLORENCE "FLO" CHADWICK (swimming)
       (Courtesy of San Diego Hall of Champions)
Below: DOROTHY HAMILL (skating)
       (Courtesy of UPI/Bettmann Newsphotos)

MILDRED "BABE" DIDRIKSON ZAHARIAS
(Above: track; courtesy of Allsport Photographic)
(Below: golf; courtesy of UPI/Bettmann Newsphotos)

Above: BILLIE JEAN KING (tennis)
            (Courtesy of UPI/Bettmann Newsphotos)
Below: NANCY LOPEZ (golf)
            (Courtesy of UPI/Bettmann Newsphotos)

Above: CHERYL MILLER (basketball)
Below: MARY LOU RETTON (gymnastics)
         (Courtesy of UPI/Bettmann Newsphotos)

Above: WILMA RUDOLPH (track)
         (Courtesy of UPI/Bettmann Newsphotos)
Below: MARY KATHRYN "MICKEY" WRIGHT (golf)
         (Courtesy of San Diego Hall of Champions)

Mary Decker sets U.S. indoor track records in the
1500-meter race (4 minutes, 0.8 second) in New York
City and the 800-meter and 880-yard races in San
Diego.

After a slow start, Donna Caponi Young regains her
top form to win the opening round of the LPGA $100,000
Corning (New York) Classic. She shoots a course
record 66 (6 under par).

Amy Alcott wins the U.S. Women's Open golf championship. She is awarded the Vare Trophy for her 71.51
scoring average, and she brings home $219,000 in
prize money for the year.

Vera Schlenker receives the WIBC 25-year participation
award.

Elvira Toepfer and Donna Adamek win the Great and
Greatest bowling titles.

Dorothea Fort is inducted into the IWBA Hall of Fame.

Dorothy Fothergill and Marge Merrick are elected to
the WIBC Hall of Fame.

Basketball twins Pam and Paula McGee from the University of Southern California try out for the U.S. Olympic
team. At 6'3", the two forwards are nicknamed the
Ebony Bookends.

Suzy Brazney is named SCAA All-League shortstop.

Nedra Jerry is named to the All-Regional and All-
Conference softball teams.

Dot Richardson bats .437 for UCLA.

Venus Jennings is named Most Valuable Player of the
Mid-Atlantic Regional Softball Tournament.

Barbara Garcia makes the AIAW All-Conference softball
team.

Marilyn Rau bats .520 in the National ASA Tournament,
leading all hitters. She also steals 24 bases.

Patty Cutright is the third leading hitter in the National ASA Tournament with an average of .450.

Wendy Hedberg plays in the ASA Nationals for the first of 3 seasons.

Pitcher Debbie Doom compiles a 42-2 record and is named Most Valuable Player in the ASA Nationals.

Jean Daves is elected to the National Softball Hall of Fame.

Betty Cook wins her second World Off Shore Racing championship in powerboating.

Rachel McLish is named the Miss Olympia of women's body building.

Jan Hansen wins her state high school championship in barrel racing.

Lynn McKenzie is the Reserve Champion Barrel Racer, winning a total of $44,678.

Donna Krening takes possession of the NFR title and becomes Rookie of the Year.

Speed skater Beth Heiden is the world champion in her sport. She also wins the world title in cycle road racing.

Linda Fratianne wins her fourth consecutive U.S. figure skating championship.

Lisa Marie Allen takes second place in the national figure skating championships.

In her first international competition, Tiffany Chin wins the women's singles title at the World Junior Figure Skating Championships in London, Ontario. She also wins the silver medal in the Junior Ladies' Division at the U.S. figure skating championships.

Bonny Warner, a varsity field hockey player for Stanford University, is a torchbearer at the Winter Olympic Games in Lake Placid. After the Games are over, she attends a two-week luge clinic to learn the sport in which she will become a pioneer for the United States.

Sharon Crawford wins her fourth consecutive U.S. orienteering championship.

1981   The first two women are elected to the 87-year-old all-male International Olympic Committee (IOC).

Doris Groves sets a new women's out and return soaring record.

Mary T. Meagher sets world swimming records in the 100- and 200-meter butterfly in Brown Deer, Wisconsin.

Melissa Belote is inducted into the Hall of Fame at Arizona State University for her swimming feats.

Ruth Caillouet is the Louisiana State Indoor and Outdoor Champion in archery for the second time.

Cindy Vezzetti wins the collegiate archery championship.

Cindy Gilbert is selected an all-American in archery.

Benita Edds is the Indoor Champion and Brown County Open Champion in archery.

Debra Metzger is named USOC Athlete of the Year in archery. She establishes a record at the National Archery Championships.

Nancy Cotton wins the national wheelchair tennis title in the Women's Open Division.

Tracy Austin wins the U.S. Open women's singles tennis title, defeating Martina Navratilova in the finals.

At age 14, Kathy Rinaldi of the United States becomes the youngest person ever to win at Wimbledon. Two days later, Rinaldi is out of the running, as she loses to Claudia Pasquale.

Chris Evert Lloyd wins the women's singles championship at Wimbledon.

The IOC votes to include a women's marathon in the
1984 Olympic Games.

Sister Marion Irvine sets the new Master World Marathon record for women 50 years of age and older with
a time of 2 hours, 55 minutes, 16.6 seconds.

At 80, Ruth Rothfarb of the United States becomes
the oldest woman to complete a marathon.

Marcy Schaum is the first American woman to complete
a 6-day running race.

Margaret Groos-Thomas sets a world indoor record
in the 5,000-meter run.

Evelyn Ashford repeats her 1979 feats, winning the
100- and 200-meter races at the World Cup Championships. She is once again voted the Woman Athlete
of the Year.

Pat Bradley is the U.S. Women's Open golf champion.

Betty Kuczynski is elected to the WIBC Hall of Fame.

Paula Weishoff and Laurie Flachmeier play for the
women's national volleyball team, of which Sue Woodstra
is the captain. The team takes fourth place in World
Cup competition and is first in the Roslock Tournament
and the North-Central and Caribbean American Championships.

Flo Hyman of the United States is selected to the All
World Cup volleyball team with five other women from
around the world.

Scoring 39 points in the final game of the championship
series, Rosie Walker leads the Nebraska Wranglers
to the Women's Professional Basketball League title.

Wende Ward is named Northern California Athletic
Conference Player of the Year in softball.

Suzy Brazney is named to the Southern California
Athletic Association (SCAA) All-League softball team.
The shortstop is voted the Most Valuable Player.

Barbara Garcia is a Western College Association (WCA)
All-Conference softball selection and receives the Most
Valuable Player award.

Chris Prieboy bats .420 for the College of St. Francis
and is named to the District 20 team. She receives
honorable mention in National Association of Intercollegiate Athletics (NAIA) All-American balloting.

Donna Michal is named to the AIAW All-Championship
softball team and is a nominee for the Broderick Cup.

Pitcher Michelle Thomas is named one of Drake University's top athletes of all time.

Monica Messmer is named Most Valuable Player in the
San Gabriel Softball League.

Sue Lewis bats .408 with 10 home runs and 47 RBIs
at California State University, Fullerton. She leads
the National Sports Festival in hitting.

Jill Larson is a Division I All-American in softball.

Brenda Gonnerman is named to the NAIA All-Tournament
softball team.

Gretchen Larson is a College All-American and an
All-Big Ten softball player.

Darlene Lowery compiles a 31-1 pitching record for
the Orlando Rebels.

Dot Richardson is named Most Valuable Player and
Outstanding Defensive Player in the ASA Nationals.

Barbara Garcia and Patty Cutright are members of
the U.S. Tri-Nation softball team that tours China
and Japan. Cutright leads the U.S. team in hitting
on the tour with a .357 average.

Carol Spanks and Shirley Topley are elected to the
National Softball Hall of Fame.

Leslie Klein is the top finisher in the women's kayak
class at the World and Pan American team trials. She

is a triple gold medalist at the Pan American Canoe
Kayak Championships; her team wins the bronze medal
at the World Whitewater Canoe/Kayak Championships;
and she captures the women's singles kayak title at the
National Marathon Canoe/Kayak Championships.

Rachel McLish is the women's professional body building
champion.

Donna Krening repeats her winning performance in
barrel racing and is named NFR Champion.

Lynn McKenzie takes fifth place and a check for $2,000
at the NFR competition.

Jan Hansen is the Reserve World Champion Barrel
Racer. With her horse, Bandit, she takes the Tur-
quoise Circuit Championship. Her horse receives
the Horse of the Year award from the top 25 barrel
racers.

Elaine Zayak wins the U.S. figure skating championship.

Lori Benton wins a bronze medal in the World University Figure Skating Championships. She is the first
American to win a medal in this competition.

Sandy Dulaney wins a gold medal in world roller skating.

Tamara McKinney skis to her first World Cup title
at the age of 18.

New Englander Sharon Crawford is the U.S. orienteering champion again.

1982   Wendy Wyland is the world champion diver in 10-meter
board competition. The 17-year-old defeats her seem-
ingly invincible Eastern European opponents at the
World Aquatic Championships in Ecuador.

Melanie Solytsik Skillman is the Pennsylvania Indoor
Archery Champion.

Janet McCullough wins the U.S. Collegiate Archery
Championship.

Ruth Rowe wins the National Archery Association Field
Championship for the second time.

Cindy Vezzetti is the Southwest Regional Archery
Champion for the first of 2 consecutive seasons.

Debra Metzger is the National Indoor Champion in
archery.

Becky Liggett places second in the Championship of
the Americas Tournament, her first international competition.

Debra J. Ochs places second at the Junior Olympic
Outdoor Nationals in archery.

Eileen Pylypchuk takes first place in the Empire State
Games and the New York State Archery Championships.

Connie Tomsovic sets a national skeet shooting record
of 379--13 higher than the previous mark.

Chris Evert Lloyd wins another U.S. Open women's
singles title.

Andrea Jaeger beats Chris Evert Lloyd for the first
time, winning the $150,000 Avon of California Tennis
Tournament.

Martina Navratilova wins the women's singles titles
at Wimbledon and the French Open.

Barbara Potter wins the Wightman Cup singles trophy
for the United States. It is the 44th American victory
in 61 years of competition.

Cheryl Carton wins the women's national badminton
title.

At San Diego, California, Mary Decker runs a mile
in 4 minutes, 20.5 seconds, setting a new U.S. indoor

record. Earlier in the year, she set U.S. indoor
records in the 2,000-meter and 3,000-meter races.
She is this year's recipient of the James E. Sullivan
Memorial Trophy.

Kathy Grimes sets a meet record for the 400-meter
hurdles at the NAIA Track Championships, winning
the event in 59.3 seconds.

Kellie Cathey of the University of Oklahoma runs 10,000
meters in 32 minutes, 22.5 seconds, setting a record
for American women.

On February 26, Evelyn Ashford sets a U.S. indoor
record for 60 yards in New York City.

Evelyn Havens is honored as the Senior Woman of
the Year by the New York Road Runners Club. In
the 4 years since she started running at age 62, she
has run 90 races and 7 marathons.

Softball player Joan Joyce tries her hand at golf.
At a tournament in Atlanta, Georgia, she records
the lowest number of putts by a woman.

JoAnne Carner is the LPGA leading money winner,
earning $310,399 for the year.

Marion Ladewig receives the BWAA's John O. Martino
Award. Brunswick holds its Memorial World Open
Bowling Tournament in her honor.

Helen Duval bowls her first perfect game just 3 days
before her 66th birthday. She is the oldest woman
to bowl 300.

Alberta E. Crowe is elected to the WIBC Hall of Fame.

Sue Woodstra captains the women's national volleyball
team to a bronze medal at the world championships.
Her teammates include Debbi Green, Rose Magers,
Sherryl Moore, Paula Weishoff, Julie Vollersten, Denise
Corlett, Linda Chisholm, Laurie Flachmeier, Rita Croc-
kett, and Tauna Vandeweghe.

Janey Rayfield sets a collegiate soccer record, scoring
93 goals in her career at the University of North Caro-
lina.

Deanna Hacker pitches Illinois Central College to a
national softball title.

Chris Prieboy bats .350 with 26 RBIs for St. Francis.
She is named to the NAIA All-Tournament team at
the softball nationals.

Brenda Gonnerman bats .441 with 9 home runs and
63 RBIs, and is named to the NAIA All-Tournament
team.

Cheryl Kay Kempf pitches Missouri Western to an NAIA
title. She is named Most Valuable Player at the tournament.

Tracie Ann Triblett is named Central Arizona College's
Most Valuable Player, compiling a 27-12 pitching record
and batting in 30 runs.

Beth Jones is the Most Valuable Softball Player at
Pittsburgh State University.

Rhonda Clark compiles a pitching record of 24-13 for
Kansas University. She pitches 2 no-hitters and 18
shutouts.

Melanie George bats .470 for Crowder College, and
is second among the nation's National Junior College
Athletic Association (NJCAA) players with 47 RBIs.

Sue Lewis of California State University, Fullerton
bats .311 with 9 home runs and 50 RBIs. She sets
4 AIAW College World Series records.

UCLA takes the NCAA Division I softball title, as
Debbie Doom pitches 9 shutouts. Dot Richardson
makes only one error for the Bruins during the entire
season, and leads the team in virtually all offensive
categories.

Suzy Brazney and Donna Mitchell are NCAA All-American
choices, as is Linda Berndt.

Marilyn Rau bats .412 at the National Sports Festival.

Wendy Hedberg, Wendy Smith, and Patty Cutright lead their Macomb Magic softball team to the ASA Nationals. Cutright takes second place in hitting with a .389 tournament average.

Jill Larson bats .400 in the ASA National Tournament.

With a 46-7 pitching record, Darlene Lowery leads the Orlando Rebels to the ASA Nationals.

Pat Dufficy bats .332 for the Raybestos Brakettes, while teammate Allyson Rioux bats .368 in the ASA Nationals.

Michelle Thomas is named Player of the Year as she gives up only 4 runs in the national softball championships.

Debbie Beacham is ranked number one woman surfer in the world by the International Professional Surfers' Association. The readers of Surfer Magazine agree, also voting her the best. She also finds time to serve as president of the Women's Professional Surfing Association.

Rachel McLish wins the Miss Olympia title and the women's professional body building championship.

Rebecca Twigg-Whitehead wins a gold medal for individual pursuit at the world championships of cycling.

Sandy Dulaney wins her second gold medal in world roller skating.

Melanie Smith wins the world championship of equestrian show jumping.

Elaine Zayak wins the world figure skating championship.

Rosalynn Sumners wins the U.S. figure skating title.

Sharon Crawford takes her sixth consecutive U.S. orienteering championship.

1983 The Swimming Hall of Fame inducts new members Melissa
Belote and Gail Johnson.

At 16, Carla Finney is the youngest competitor at
the Archery Sports Festival.

Sandra Elaine Christensen is the Southern Indoor
and Outdoor Archery Champion.

Rebecca Wallace is the National Collegiate Champion
in archery and a member of the Pan American team.

Melanie Solytsik Skillman takes second place at the
Mid-Atlantic Indoor Archery Competition.

Tricia Green is the Southeastern Archery Champion.

Ruth Rowe is the U.S. Indoor Archery Champion.

Debra J. Ochs is the Junior Olympic Indoor Champion
and the National Indoor Intermediate Champion in archery.

Luann Ryon becomes the National Champion in archery
for the fourth time. She also holds the top position
on the national archery team.

Elaine Carlson, injured during her career as a police
sergeant, wins 5 medals for air weapons and 7 gold
medals for various sports at the Far West Wheelchair
Games.

Teresa Spoulos, with only 1/15 of normal eyesight in
one eye, wins gold and silver medals in powerlifting
at the National Championships for the Blind.

Martina Navratilova wins women's singles tennis titles
at the U.S. Open and Wimbledon. With partner Pam
Shriver, she also takes first place in women's doubles
competition at the U.S. Open.

Pam Shriver wins America's 45th match in Wightman
Cup tennis.

Chris Evert Lloyd is the women's singles champion at
the French Open tennis tournament.

Cheryl Carton wins her fourth national women's badminton title.

In the Boston Marathon, Joan Benoit finishes in 2 hours, 22 minutes, 42 seconds, the fastest time ever for a woman.

Evelyn Ashford sets a world indoor record for the 50-yard dash (5.74 seconds) at the San Diego Indoor Games.

Stephanie Hightower sets U.S. indoor records in the 60-meter hurdles and the 60-yard hurdles.

Judi Brown King wins the NCAA 400-meter hurdle race.

Mary Decker wins the 1500- and 3,000-meter races at the World Championships of Track and Field in Helsinki. She holds 7 American records for distances ranging from 800 through 10,000 meters, and she is undefeated in 20 finals this year. Sports Illustrated names her Sportswoman of the Year.

Nancy Cotton wins the 200- and 400-meter races at the National Wheelchair Games in Hawaii. She takes second place in the 100-meter race and is a member of the silver-medal-winning 4 × 100 relay team. She has competed in 2 half-marathons this year.

Jan Stephenson is the U.S. Women's Open golf champion.

Patty Sheehan wins the LPGA championship and is named LPGA Player of the Year.

JoAnne Carner repeats as the leading LPGA money winner.

Patty Dowdell rejoins the U.S. women's national volleyball team after a 3-year leave.

Cheryl Miller, USC basketball player, is named a Kodak All-American. She leads her team to victory in the NCAA championships and is voted the tournament's Most Valuable Player.

Soccer goalie Joan Sutherland of Pacific Lutheran University is responsible for her team's 11th straight shutout victory.

Debbie Doom and Deanna Hacker compile identical shutout records of 15 in softball. Doom fans 193 batters in 147 innings.

Brenda Gonnerman is named to the All-Conference and All-District softball teams.

Mary L. Ross is selected to the all-American team for the ASA Nationals.

Linda Kae James is a member of the American team at the fifth Women's World Softball Championships in Taipei.

Pitcher Kathy Van Wyk receives the Broderick Award.

Jacquie Phelan is the National Off-Road Bicycle Association champion.

Rosalynn Sumners takes first place at the U.S. and world figure skating championships.

Tiffany Chin of Toluca Lake, California, places third in national figure skating competition.

Tamara McKinney becomes the first American woman to win the World Cup Skiing Championship at Vail, Colorado.

Debi Pelletier, also known as "Killer Tomato," makes her professional wrestling debut.

1984   Twelve-year-old Wendy Molitor is one of the torch-bearers for the XXIInd Olympiad in Los Angeles. Paralyzed from the neck down, she negotiates her section of the route in a wheelchair.

Mary T. Meagher sets Olympic swimming records in the 100- and 200-meter butterfly.

Carrie Steinseifer and Nancy Hogshead tie for the
Olympic gold medal in the 100-meter freestyle. It
is the first dead heat in Olympic swimming competition.

Mary Wayte wins the 200-meter Olympic freestyle swimming competition.

Tiffany Cohen wins the 400- and 800-meter Olympic
freestyle competitions.

Tracy Caulkins wins the 200- and 400-meter individual
medleys, setting an Olympic swimming record in the
200-meter race.

Theresa Andrews takes the Olympic gold medal in
the 100-meter backstroke.

Tracie Ruiz wins the solo synchronized swimming event
at the Olympics. She and partner Candy Costie are
the gold-medal-winning duet.

Pat Spurgin takes the Olympic gold medal in air rifle
competition.

Martina Navratilova wins the grand slam of women's
tennis, setting a single season earnings record of
$2,173,556. In addition to winning the women's sin-
gles competitions at Wimbledon, the French Open,
the U.S. Open, and the Australian Open, she and
partner Pam Shriver win the women's doubles titles
at Wimbledon and Forest Hills.

Dorothy May Bundy-Cheney ends her 43-year tennis
career in which she has won 141 American titles.

Vicky Nelson and Jean Hepner, in a 6-hour, 22-minute
tennis match in Richmond, Virginia, stage the longest
rally in women's tennis. The ball goes over the net
643 times!

Joan Benoit wins the first Olympic marathon ever held
for women with a time of 2 hours, 24 minutes, 52
seconds.

Evelyn Ashford wins 3 gold medals, setting Olympic

and world records for the 100-meter run in women's
track and field. In her final 100 meters of the Olympic relay event, she achieves a speed of 22.5 mph--
the fastest speed attained from a running start in
women's track.

Valerie Brisco-Hooks sets Olympic track records, winning the 200- and 400-meter events.

Benita Brown-Fitzgerald wins the Olympic 100-meter
hurdles.

Judi Brown King wins a silver medal in the 400-meter
hurdles.

Julie McNamara wins the Olympic gold medal for uneven
parallel bars competition in gymnastics.

American teammate Mary Lou Retton takes the Olympic
gold medal for all-around gymnastics competition.

On August 24, Pat Bradley sets an LPGA record in
Denver, Colorado, using only 28 strokes for 9 holes.

Hollis Stacy wins her third U.S. Women's Open golf
tournament.

Patty Sheehan wins the LPGA championship.

Beth Beglin, Sheryl Johnson, and Marcy Place von
Schottenstein lead the U.S. women's field hockey team
to a third place finish in Olympic competition.

Annette Kennedy of the State University of New York
at Purchase scores a record 70 points in a basketball
game against Pratt Institute.

Cheryl Miller, USC's Kodak All-American, is the leading scorer on the American gold-medal-winning basketball team. Her other honors for the year include
the Naismith Player of the Year Award, the Broderick
Cup, and the NCAA Tournament Most Valuable Player
Award.

Valerie Fons and Verlen Kruger canoe 2,552 miles
down the Mississippi River in 128 days.

Mary Schmidt and Bev Gordon canoe 3,810 miles down the Mississippi and Missouri Rivers in 98 days.

The women's 8-member crew wins the first Olympic gold medal for American women in rowing competition.

Mary Ryan sets a world power lifting record, bench pressing 95 kilograms.

Majik Jones lifts 625 kilograms, setting a world power lifting record in the squat.

Vicki Steenrod, in a lift of 475 kilograms, sets world records in her weight class for the squat, bench press, and dead lift.

Ruthi Shafer sets a world power lifting record for her weight class in the dead lift--244 kilograms.

Corinna Everson is Ms. Olympia and also the national women's body building champion.

Connie Carpenter-Phinney wins the individual road race in Olympic cycling.

Rebecca Twigg-Whitehead wins the gold medal for individual pursuit at the world championships of cycling.

Jacquie Phelan wins the National Off-Road Bicycle Association championship.

Rosalynn Sumners wins the U.S. figure skating championship.

Tiffany Chin places second in national figure skating competition. At the Winter Olympics, she places second in the freestyle skating program and fourth overall.

In Les Arcs, France, Melissa Dimino skis at 124.759 miles per hour, the highest downhill speed ever achieved by a woman.

Debbie Armstrong takes the Olympic gold medal in the women's giant slalom.

Tamara McKinney of Lexington, Kentucky, wins the
world slalom title.

Bonny Warner finishes 15th in Olympic luge competition,
equaling the best performance ever by an American
woman.

Sharon Crawford, a native New Englander, wins the
U.S. orienteering championship.

1985 New York City native Judy Horowitz sets a frisbee
throwing record of 196.9 feet at La Mirada, California.

Julie Ridge, a New York actress, swims around Man-
hattan in 6 days--the longest swim ever around Man-
hattan Island.

Martina Navratilova is the women's singles champion
at Wimbledon and takes second place at Forest Hills.

Kathy Jordan and Liz Smylie team up to win the wom-
en's doubles competition at Wimbledon.

Chris Evert Lloyd wins the Wightman Cup and the
women's singles title at the French Open. From 1971
to 1985, she has not lost a singles match. The Wom-
en's Sports Foundation declares her the Greatest American Woman Athlete of the Last 25 Years.

The James E. Sullivan Memorial Trophy goes to mara-
thoner Joan Benoit Samuelson.

Mary Decker Slaney sets a world track record for
women in Zurich, Switzerland, running the mile in
4 minutes, 16.71 seconds.

On February 22, Valerie Brisco-Hooks sets the U.S.
indoor 110-yard record.

On March 2, Joetta Clark sets the U.S. indoor record
in the 500-meter run.

Nancy Lopez earns $416,472 in golf tournament play,
setting a single season record.

In her 23rd year on the LPGA tour, Kathy Whitworth
wins her 88th match, more tournament victories than
any other woman golfer.

Kathy Baker wins the U.S. Women's Open golf championship.

Annette Alverson of Ohio Northern University hits a
field goal from 72 feet, 6 inches--the longest distance
ever in women's basketball.

USC star Cheryl Miller continues her success story
in women's basketball, winning her second Naismith
Player of the Year Award, her third Kodak All-American
Award, plus trophies as the Wade Player of the Year
and the Champion Player of the Year.

Karyn Tarter lifts 303 pounds overhead in clean-and-
jerk weight lifting competition, breaking Kate Sand-
wina's record of 286 pounds that was set in 1911.

Cheryl Jones lifts 350 kilograms, setting a world power
lifting record for her weight class.

Corinna Everson wins her second Ms. Olympia body
building title.

Susan Notorangelo cycles 3,120.2 miles across the
United States in 10 days, 14 hours, 25 minutes.

Rebecca Twigg-Whitehead wins her third gold medal
for individual pursuit at the world championships of
cycling.

Jacquie Phelan wins her third consecutive National
Off-Road Bicycle Association championship.

Lyn St. James records the fastest average lap for
a woman on a closed-circuit race track. Using a Mus-
tang Probe, she achieves a speed of 204.223 miles per
hour.

Tiffany Chin wins the U.S. figure skating championship.

Figure skater Jill Trenary's calf muscle is severed
by another skater's blade. It is feared that she will
never walk--or skate--again.

Anna Marie Danks and her partner win the silver
medal in roller skate dancing competition at the world
championships.

Sharon Crawford repeats as the U.S. orienteering
champion.

1986 Diane Benjamin is the first woman to be an athletic
trainer for a professional basketball team. She is
employed by the Charleston Gunners.

Candace Cablebrookes wins the Wheels of Fire 15-
kilometer wheelchair race in Seattle, Washington.
Twenty-eight women compete in the event.

On June 27, Betsy Mitchell sets the world record for
the 200-meter backstroke in Orlando, Florida.

Megan Neyer wins the 1-meter and 3-meter competitions
at the U.S. diving championships.

Michele Mitchell takes first place in platform competition
at the U.S. diving championships.

Karen E. Monez excels in small-bore rifle shooting,
capturing the women's small-bore rifle 3-position and
4-position titles in addition to the open small-bore
rifle title at the National Indoor Rifle and Pistol Championships.

Mary L. Godlove takes the small-bore rifle international
and air rifle titles at the National Indoor Rifle and
Pistol Championships.

Gloria K. Parmentier wins the women's small-bore rifle
international competition at the National Indoor Rifle
and Pistol Championships.

Joyce A. Myers wins the women's small-bore rifle

3-position title at the National Outdoor Rifle and Pistol Championships.

At the National Outdoor Rifle and Pistol Championships, Nancy H. Gallagher wins the individual women's high-power rifle competition.

Pat Spurgin takes the women's standard rifle 3-position title at the U.S. NRA International Shooting Championships.

Deena L. Wigger wins the women's standard rifle prone title at the U.S. NRA International Shooting Championships.

Elaine S. Proffitt wins the women's air rifle title at the U.S. NRA International Shooting Championships.

Judith L. Kemp wins the women's air pistol title at the U.S. NRA International Shooting Championships. She wins the same title, plus the women's international standard pistol championships, at the National Indoor Rifle and Pistol Championships.

Ruby E. Fox wins the women's sport pistol title at the U.S. NRA International Shooting Championships.

Meredith Flynn wins the women's conventional pistol competition at the National Indoor Rifle and Pistol Championships.

Lori B. Kamler wins the women's international free pistol title at the National Indoor Rifle and Pistol Championships.

By the end of the year, Martina Navratilova has earned a total of $11,488,658 in her tennis career. She wins the women's singles titles at Wimbledon and Forest Hills en route to 1,000 career victories.

Pam Shriver teams up with Martina Navratilova to win the doubles competition at the U.S. Open.

Chris Evert Lloyd takes the Federation Cup in women's tennis and wins the French Open, but ends her string of consecutive singles victories.

Nikki Willette and her brother Sean win the 18-and-under brother-and-sister doubles competition at the Equitable Family Tennis Challenge. Their mother is former tennis star Kathy Chabot Willette.

Alicia McConnell wins her fifth women's singles squash racquets championship.

Lynn Adams completes an undefeated season in women's racquetball. In the 15-year history of the sport, she is the first professional to finish an entire season without a loss.

Jackie Joyner accumulates 7,161 points in the heptathlon, setting a world track and field record for women. She breaks the existing U.S. indoor long jump record, jumping 22 feet, 10 1/2 inches. She is the recipient of the Jesse Owens Award for the top American track and field athlete and the James E. Sullivan Award as well.

On February 28, Stephanie Hightower runs the 60-yard hurdles in 7.44 seconds at the USA/Mobil indoor track and field championships.

At the USA/Mobil outdoor track and field championships, Pam Marshall wins the 100- and 200-meter races.

Joetta Clark breaks existing American records for the 1,000-yard and 1,000-meter runs in Gainesville, Florida.

Yolande Mavity wins the U.S. gymnastics floor exercise competition.

Angie Denkins takes first place in balance beam competition at the U.S. gymnastics meet.

Marie Roethlisberger is the U.S. gymnastics uneven parallel bars champion.

Joyce Phillips takes first place in vaulting at the U.S. gymnastics meet.

Jennifer Sey is the U.S. all-around gymnastics champion.

At 95+ years, Erna Ross is the oldest woman to score a hole in one. She accomplishes her feat on the 17th green of the Everglades Club Golf Course at Palm Beach, Florida.

Pat Bradley sets a new season money record for women golfers, running her LPGA career total to $2,283,946. She is named the Rolex Player of the Year.

Jane Geddes is the U.S. Women's Open golf champion.

Mary Covell bowls in her 55th WIBC tournament.

At the age of 98, Ethel Brunnick is the oldest WIBC tournament bowler.

Dana Stewart of Morgan Hill, California, wins the WIBC individual championship with a total score of 698.

Californians Robin Romeo and Maria Lewis tie for the WIBC all-events title. They each knock down a total of 1,877 pins.

Sally Gates and Marilyn Frazier, also of California, win the WIBC 2-woman team bowling competition.

Jeanne Maiden bowls 40 strikes in a row. She also rolls 11 300-point games for a new WIBC record.

Patty Ann sets a record with her season bowling average of 227.

Nina Matthies and Linda Robertson win 7 of 8 beach volleyball tournaments on the pro circuit. They are the top women's team in the country. Nina makes $8,000, while top men in the sport earn $100,000.

The Tampa Bay Little League All-Stars win the 11-to-12-year-old girls' Little League World Series of softball.

Barbara Cleveland wins the senior women's slalom, jump, and overall waterskiing titles at the National Waterski Championship in West Palm Beach, Florida.

Thelma Salmas wins the senior women's waterskiing tricks competition at West Palm Beach.

Deena Brush is the women's tricks, jump, and overall waterskiing champion at West Palm Beach. In the Masters Water Ski Tournament, she wins the women's jump and overall competitions.

Kristi Overton takes the girls' tricks, jump, and overall waterskiing titles at West Palm Beach. In addition, she wins the women's tricks competition in the Masters Water Ski Tournament.

Julie Shull wins the girls' slalom title at the National Waterski Championship.

Kim Laskoff is the women's slalom waterskiing champion at West Palm Beach.

At Callaway Gardens, Georgia, Camille Duvall takes the women's slalom title in the Masters Water Ski Tournament.

Corinna Everson wins her third Ms. Olympia body building title.

Laura Creavalle of California wins the U.S. body building championship.

Cathey Palzo wins the amateur heavyweight and national women's body building championship.

Elaine Mariolle rides 3,107.3 miles across the United States in 10 hours, 2 days, 4 minutes, setting a new cycling record.

Charmayne James earns a record $151,969 in women's rodeo barrel racing.

Debi Thomas, a premed student at Stanford University, wins both the U.S. and the world figure skating championships.

Caryn Kadavy of Erie, Pennsylvania, takes second place in the U.S. figure skating championships.

Jill Trenary of Minnetonka, Minnesota, finishes fifth in women's national figure skating competition.

Leslie Krichko shows her versatility by sweeping the Nordic Skiing Championships, winning a medal in the national masters rowing competition finals, and taking first place in the "Pole, Pedal and Paddle" contest in Bend, Oregon.

With five men and a dogsled, Ann Bancroft is the first woman to reach the North Pole. The journey takes 56 days to complete.

Cammy Myler is the first American to win a medal in World Cup luge competition. She takes third place.

Once again, New Englander Sharon Crawford is the U.S. orienteering champion.

1987   Sports Illustrated selects 2 women and 6 men as Sportswomen and Sportsmen of the Year. All of the chosen athletes excel in their respective sports, but all have one additional quality in common: a devotion to organizations that help children. These athletes "best practice the ideals of sportsmanship away from the arena" (Deford 1987, 15).

Golfer Patty Sheehan is selected as one of the Sports Illustrated Sportswomen of the Year for her work with troubled adolescent girls.

Track star Judi Brown King wins the 400-meter hurdle competition at the Pan American Games, breaking her own American record. She is honored as one of the Sports Illustrated Sportswomen of the Year for her work with abused children.

Janet Evans sets world records in the 800- and 1500-meter freestyle competitions at the U.S. long course national swimming championships. She also sets a world record in the 400-meter freestyle at the U.S. Open.

With a time of 2 minutes, 29.78 seconds, Amy Shaw

becomes the first American woman to break 2 1/2 minutes in the 200-meter breaststroke. She sets the
record at the U.S. long course nationals.

At age 56, Ann Pisciotta wins 6 gold medals for her
age group at the Masters short course national swimming competition.

Megan Neyer takes first place in American outdoor
1-meter diving competition. She also wins the 3-
meter competition at the U.S. indoor championships.

Kelly McCormick wins the 3-meter springboard diving
titles at the U.S. outdoor championships and the Pan
American Games.

Mary Ellen Clark takes first place in platform diving
at the U.S. outdoor championships.

Kim Fugett wins the 1-meter indoor competition.

Michele Miller places first in platform diving at the
U.S. indoor championships.

Tracie Ruiz-Conforto wins the gold medal for solo
synchronized swimming at the Pan American Games.

Karen and Sarah Josephson win the gold medal as the
best synchronized swimming duet at the Pan American
Games.

Denise Parker of South Jordan, Utah, wins the Junior
Archery Championship of the U.S. and a gold medal
at the Pan Am Games. At 14, she is the youngest
competitor to win a gold medal in any Pan American
sport.

Cary Quinn wins her first archery title, taking the
national target championship.

Connie Fluker wins the U.S. international skeet shooting championship.

Launi Meili wins the U.S. NRA international air rifle
competition.

Ruby E. Fox wins the women's pistol title at the
National Outdoor Rifle and Pistol Championships.

Gwendolyn H. Fox wins the women's small-bore rifle
prone competition at the National Outdoor Rifle and
Pistol Championships.

Karen E. Monez wins the open and women's competition
in small-bore rifle 3-position shooting at the National
Outdoor Rifle and Pistol Championships.

Kathy M. Livingstone wins the women's high-power
rifle competition at the National Outdoor Rifle and
Pistol Championships.

Mary L. Godlove takes the women's standard rifle
prone title at the U.S. NRA International Shooting
Championships.

Deena L. Wigger wins the women's standard rifle 3-
position championship at the U.S. NRA competition.

At the National Indoor Rifle and Pistol Championships,
Denise L. Loring wins the women's small-bore rifle
4-position title.

Wanda R. Jewell wins two events at the National Indoor
Rifle and Pistol Championships: the women's small-
bore rifle international and the women's small-bore
rifle 3-position contests.

Judith L. Kemp takes two indoor titles: the women's
conventional and the women's international standard
pistol competitions.

Pat Spurgin wins the women's air rifle title at the
National Indoor Rifle and Pistol Championships.

Martina Navratilova continues her successful tradition
at Wimbledon, winning her eighth tennis singles title
(her sixth in a row). She also wins the Virginia
Slims Championship and the singles competition at the
U.S. Open. With partner Pam Shriver, she takes
the doubles title at Forest Hills as well.

Pam Shriver is the fourth-ranked woman tennis player
in the world and the fourth leading money winner
for the year.

Insook Bhushan of Aurora, Colorado, wins her eighth
national women's table tennis title. She repeats her
performance as Pan American singles champion.

Four-time Olympian Martha Watson is elected to the
National Track and Field Hall of Fame. Although her
best Olympic performance was tenth place in the long
jump in Mexico City, she won the U.S. national indoor
long jump championship 5 times and the outdoor title
3 times.

Jackie Joyner-Kersee wins her second Jesse Owens
Award as the top track and field athlete in America.
She ties the women's world long jump record (24 feet,
5 1/2 inches) at the Pan American Games and wins
the long jump and heptathlon events at the world
championships in Rome.

American women take gold medals in the 3,000-meter,
1500-meter, and 10-kilometer track and field events
at the Pan American Games in Indianapolis. Mary
Knisely wins the 3,000-meter; Linda Sheskey takes
the 1500-meter; and Marty Cooksey sets a Pan Am
record in the 10-kilometer, beating her favored Canadian opponent.

San Antonio native Kimberly Arata wins her fourth
straight U.S. modern pentathlon title (her sixth overall). She finishes tenth in the World Ladies' Championships in Bensheim, West Germany.

Sheila Hudson's triple jump of 45 feet, 2 1/2 inches
is a new world outdoor record for women.

Yvette Bates of the University of Southern California
jumps 45 feet, 3 inches at the NCAA indoor championships.

Jeanine Radice, a junior at Fordham University, takes
time out from her basketball schedule to win the

Metropolitan Intercollegiate Women's Cross Country
title.   She runs 3.1 miles in 18 minutes, 15 seconds.

Lynn Jennings wins The Athletics Congress-USA Cross
Country Championship in running with a time of 19
minutes, 35 seconds for 3.7 miles.   She places sixth
in the women's 10,000-meter race at the world championships in Rome.

Indiana University sophomore Kim Betz is the NCAA
women's cross-country champion.

Gwen Torrence sets a world record at the NCAA indoor
championships, running 55 meters in 6.56 seconds.
She also wins the 60-yard dash at the Millrose Games
and the 100- and 200-meter competitions at the NCAA
outdoor championships.

Joetta Clark takes first place in the 800-meter run
at the Millrose Games.

Debbi Waldear wins the San Diego Marathon, setting
a personal record of 2 hours, 50 minutes, 49 seconds.

Jeanne Lasse-Johnson takes second place in the San
Diego Marathon, completing the course in 2 hours,
52 minutes, 5 seconds.

Maureen Custy wins the Women's Holiday Bowl Marathon
in San Diego with a time of 2 hours, 33 minutes, 38
seconds--the fastest run by an American woman this
year.

Kirsten Hanssen of Denver is the Bud Light U.S.
Triathlon Series Women's Champion.

Mary Hammes, a Fort Worth, Texas, native, wins the
Western States Ultra-Marathon, one of the most gruel-
ing tests of endurance in sports.

Sabrina Mar wins 5 gold medals, including the all-
around title, in Pan American gymnastics competition.

Diane Simpson takes 4 gold medals in rhythmic gymnastics at the Pan American Games.

Kristie Phillips of Baton Rouge, Louisiana, wins the women's title at the U.S. Gymnastics Championships.

Laura Davies wins the U.S. Women's Open golf tournament.

Nancy Lopez and her partner take the $850,000 Mazda Champions Golf Tournament.

Jane Geddes takes first place in the LPGA tournament and is the third leading money winner for the year.

At the first women's professional doubles bowling tournament, Jeanne Berry and Tish Johnson win $7,000 each.

Albuquerque native Pam Hollander bowls the first 800 series ever by a woman in New Mexico. Her three scores are 269, 247, and 288, for a total of 804 pins.

In a bowling marathon, Diane Mahon-Westmoreland rolls 150 games in 17 hours, 22 minutes.

Lynne Stever, a senior forward on the Nazareth College women's soccer team, scores 5 goals in a game against Utica College. Her career scoring total soars to 95, a new collegiate record.

Soccer goalie Gail Stenzel of Pacific Lutheran University chalks up her 11th consecutive shutout.

Sheryl Johnson of Fremont, California, scores 5 goals in 5 games as she leads the U.S. national women's field hockey team to a silver medal at the Pan American Games.

Nancy Lieberman, who started her professional career with the Dallas Diamonds of the Women's Basketball Association, now plays with the Washington Generals, the team that travels with the Harlem Globetrotters.

Lynette Woodard decides to leave the Harlem Globetrotters after 2 seasons because of a contract dispute. She says she is not free to pursue "outside interests ... 'such as endorsements'" (Long Beach Press Telegram, October 24, 1987, sports section).

Tresa Spauling of Brigham Young University leads
Division I scorers in NCAA basketball with a 28.9
average. Division II and III leaders are Theresa
Lorenzi of Bloomsburg State and Jeannie Demers of
Buena Vista. Mary McCullom of William Carey aver-
ages 32.1 points per game to lead the NAIA.

Cheryl Myers sets a new basketball record, shooting
and making a field goal from 77 feet.

The Baseball Hall of Fame in Cooperstown, New York,
announces its decision to honor women who played
professional baseball between 1943 and 1954. The
special exhibit, tentatively scheduled for 1989, will
honor women who played in the All-American Girls'
Professional Baseball League. Lillian "Tennessee"
Jackson and Marie "Red" Mahoney will be among the
honorees.

Pam Postema, an umpire in professional baseball's
American Association, may move up to the major leagues
in 1988, after 11 seasons in the minor leagues.

The Tampa Bay Little League All-Stars win the 11
to 12-year-old girls' Little League World Series of
softball for the second year in a row.

Jean Schley Campbell, a 1973 Smith College graduate,
represents the United States in the world championships for white-water canoeing and kayaking.

Kim Laskoff wins the women's slalom competition at
the world waterskiing championships.

Deena Brush wins the jump and overall titles at the
world waterskiing championships. She sets a women's
jump record with a distance of 150 feet, 11 inches.
She also wins the women's jump and overall competitions at the Masters Water Ski Tournament and the
U.S. Open.

Camille Duvall wins the women's slalom competition
at the Masters Water Ski Tournament.

Karyn Marshall of Pelham, New York, wins the 181.75-

pound weight lifting title at the first Women's World
Championships. She lifts a total of 485 pounds--
209.4 in the snatch and 275.6 in the clean and jerk.

Rebecca Twigg-Whitehead wins gold medals in Pan
American road race and pursuit cycling. She also
wins a gold medal for individual pursuit at the world
championships.

Kate Harvey wins the Good Hands Finals, the Challenge
Cup, and the American Royal Equestrian Medal Finals.
She is the third rider to win the "triple crown" of
saddle-seat equitation.

Julie Krone, at 100 pounds, is the first female jockey
to lead at 2 major tracks in the same year. She takes
the titles at Monmouth and the Meadowlands, winning
a total of 124 races at the latter track.

Speed skater Bonnie Blair sets a world record in 500-
meter competition.

On December 6, Bonnie Blair loses her world record
at Calgary, Canada, but she wins 4 medals at the
World Cup speed skating competition. She takes a
first and a second place in the 500-meter; a second
place in the 1,000, when she sets a U.S. record;
and a third place in the 1500. She wins her fifth
1,000-meter race in 1 minute, 24.27 seconds at the
U.S. Olympic speed skating trials in Milwaukee on
December 14.

Leslie Bader takes first place in the 3,000-meter race
in 4 minutes, 44.85 seconds at the U.S. Olympic speed
skating trials.

Leslie Docter, a 2-time Olympian from Madison, Wisconsin, takes second place in the women's 3,000-meter
race at the U.S. Olympic speed skating trials.

Jill Trenary wins the U.S. figure skating championship.

Debi Thomas records second-place finishes in both
the U.S. and the world figure skating championships.

Caryn Kadavy takes third place at the national figure
skating championships.

Olympian Tiffany Chin turns pro, signing a 2-year,
$1 million contract with Holiday on Ice. She will also
guest star on the Ice Capades.

Because of a hairline fracture of her lower left leg,
skier Tamara McKinney may miss 10 World Cup races.
She is still scheduled to compete in the 1988 Olympics.

Bonny Warner of Mt. Baldy, California, finishes fifth
in the World Luge Championship in Austria.
The only American to win a luge race at Lake Placid,
New York, she ties for third place in the overall wom-
en's World Cup standings.

Susan Butcher wins her second straight Iditarod Trail
sled dog race, traveling 1,138 miles from Anchorage
to Nome, Alaska.

With a background of 8 years in sports, Gayle Sierens
is the first woman broadcaster to do play-by-play
for an NFL game.

Gayle Gardner is scheduled to host the Fiesta, Rose,
and Orange Bowls for NBC television on New Year's
Day, 1988.

REFERENCES

Books and Articles

Adler, Larry. 1978. Young Women in the World of Race Horses. New York: David McKay.

Baker, Jim. 1974. Billie Jean King. New York: Grosset & Dunlap.

Batten, Jack. 1971. Champions. Toronto: New Press.

Berke, Art, ed. 1974. The Lincoln Library of Sports Champions. Vols. 11-14. Columbus, Ohio: Sports Resources.

Besford, Pat. 1976. Encyclopaedia of Swimming. 2nd ed. New York: St. Martin's Press.

Borstein, Larry. 1978. After Olympic Glory. New York: Warne.

Brown, Fern G. 1976. Racing against the Odds: Robyn G. Smith. Milwaukee: Raintree Editions.

Burchard, Marshall, and Sue H. Burchard. 1975. Sports Hero: Billie Jean King. New York: G. P. Putnam's Sons.

Burchard, Sue H. 1978. Sports Star: Dorothy Hamill. New York: Harcourt Brace Jovanovich.

_____. 1976. Chris Evert. New York: Harcourt Brace Jovanovich.

Butcher, Grace. 1976. Women in Sports: Motorcycling. New York: Harvey House.

119

Calhoun, Don. 1981. Sports, Culture and Personality.
Berkeley, Calif.: Leisure Press.

Campbell, Gail. 1977. Marathon: The World of the Long-
Distance Athlete. New York: Sterling.

Connolly, Olga. 1968. The Rings of Destiny. New York:
David McKay.

Davenport, Joanna. 1978. "The Women's Movement into
the Olympic Games." Journal of Physical Education and
Recreation (March): 58-60.

Davidson, Owen, and C. M. Jones. 1971. Great Women
Tennis Players. London: Pelham Books.

Deford, Frank. 1987. "A Little Lower than the Angels."
Sports Illustrated 67(27): 12-15 [sportswomen and
sportsmen of 1987].

Dolan, Edward F., Jr., and Richard B. Lyttle. 1978. Janet
Guthrie, First Woman Driver at Indianapolis. Garden City,
N.Y.: Doubleday.

_____. 1977. Martina Navratilova. Garden City, N.Y.:
Doubleday.

Donovan, Hedley, ed. 1976. Chris Evert: Princess of
Tennis. Mankato, Minn.: Crestwood House.

_____. 1976. Cindy Nelson: North Country Skier. St.
Paul: EMC.

_____. 1976. Forest Hills and the American Tennis Cham-
pionship. Mankato, Minn.: Creative Education.

_____. 1976. Remarkable American Women, 1776-1976.
Life Special Report. New York: Time-Life Books.

Elliot, Len, and Barbara Kelly. 1976. Who's Who in Golf.
New Rochelle, N.Y.: Arlington House.

Emery, David, and Stan Greenberg. 1986. World Sports
Record Atlas. New York: Facts on File.

_____; retold by John Kenneth. 1973. Lillian. London:
Blackie & Son.

Francis, Clare. 1977. Come Hell or High Water. London:
Pelham Books [sailing].

_____. 1977. Woman Alone. New York: David McKay.

Gemme, Leila B. 1976. King on the Court: Billie Jean King.
Milwaukee: Raintree Editions.

_____. 1975. The New Breed of Athlete. New York:
Pocket Books.

Gerber, Ellen W. 1971. Innovators and Institutions in Physical Education. Philadelphia: Lea & Febiger.

_____, Jan Felshin, Pearl Berlin, and Waneen Wyrick.
1974. The American Woman in Sport. Reading, Mass.:
Addison-Wesley.

Gibson, Althea, with Richard Curtis. 1968. So Much to
Live For. New York: G. P. Putnam's Sons.

Gleasner, Diana C. 1977. Women in Sports: Track and
Field. New York: Harvey House.

_____. 1975. Women in Sports: Swimming. New York:
Harvey House.

Glickman, William G. 1978. Winners on the Tennis Court.
New York: Franklin Watts.

Golden, Flora. 1978. Women in Sports: Horseback Riding.
New York: Harvey House.

Green, Tina Sloan, Carole A. Oglesby, Alpha Alexander, and
Nikki Franke. 1981. Black Women in Sport. Reston, Va.:
American Alliance for Health, Physical Education, Recrea-
tion, and Dance.

Grimsley, Will, ed. 1971. The Sports Immortals. Englewood
Cliffs, N.J.: Prentice-Hall.

Gutman, Bill. 1977. Modern Women Superstars. New York:
Dodd, Mead.

Hahn, James, and Lynn Hahn. 1979. Janet Guthrie: Champion Racer. St. Paul: EMC.

_____. 1979. Nancy Lopez: Golfing Pioneer. St. Paul: EMC.

_____. 1978. Tracy Austin: Powerhouse in Pinafore. St. Paul: EMC.

Haney, Lynn. 1976. Chris Evert, the Young Champion. New York: G. P. Putnam's Sons.

_____. 1973. The Lady Is a Jock. New York: Dodd, Mead.

Hanley, Reid M. 1973. Who's Who in Track and Field. New Rochelle, N.Y.: Arlington House.

Henry, Bill, and Patricia Henry Yeomans. 1984. An Approved History of the Olympic Games. Sherman Oaks, Calif.: Alfred Publishing.

Higdon, Hal. 1971. Champions of the Tennis Court. Englewood Cliffs, N.J.: Prentice-Hall.

Hoffman, Mark S., ed. 1988. The World Almanac and Book of Facts 1988. New York: Pharos Books.

Hollander, Phyllis. 1972. American Women in Sports. New York: Grosset & Dunlap.

Houser, Hillary. 1976. Women in Sports: Scuba Diving. New York: Harvey House.

Howell, Reet. 1982. Her Story in Sport. West Point, N.Y.: Leisure Press.

Huey, Lynda. 1976. A Running Start. New York: Quadrangle [track and field].

Jackson, Madeline Manning, as told to Jerry B. Jenkins. 1977. Running for Jesus. Waco, Tex.: Word.

Jacobs, Helen Hull. 1975. Famous Modern American Women Athletes. New York: Dodd, Mead.

_____. 1970. Gallery of Champions. Freeport, N.Y.: Books for Libraries Press.

Jacobs, Karen Folger. 1978. Girlsports. New York: Bantam Books.

Jacobs, Linda. 1976. Madeline Manning Jackson: Running on Faith. St. Paul: EMC.

_____. 1976. Robyn Smith: In Silks. St. Paul: EMC.

_____. 1975. Cathy Rigby: On the Beam. St. Paul: EMC.

_____. 1975. Joan Moore Rice: The Olympic Dream. St. Paul: EMC.

_____. 1975. Laura Baugh: Golf's Golden Girl. St. Paul: EMC.

_____. 1974. Chris Evert: Tennis Pro. St. Paul: EMC.

_____. 1974. Janet Lynn: Sunshine on Ice. St. Paul: EMC.

James, Edward T., ed. 1971. Notable American Women, 1607-1950: A Biographical Dictionary. Cambridge: Harvard University Press, Belknap Press.

Johnson, William O., and Nancy Williamson. 1977. Whatta Gal! The Babe Didrikson Story. Boston: Little, Brown.

Jones, Ann. 1971. A Game to Love. London: Stanley Paul.

Jordan, Pat. 1977. Broken Patterns. New York: Dodd, Mead [track and field].

King, Billie Jean, with Kim Chapin. 1975. Billie Jean. London: W. H. Allen.

Krementz, Jill. 1978. A Very Young Gymnast. New York: Alfred A. Knopf.

_____. 1978. A Very Young Rider. New York: Alfred A. Knopf.

Lee, Mabel. 1978. Memories beyond Bloomers, 1924-1954.
     Washington: AAHPER.

_____. 1977. Memories of a Bloomer Girl, 1894-1924.
     Washington: AAHPER.

Leipold, L. Edmond. 1969. Famous American Athletes.
     Minneapolis: T. S. Denison.

Leslie, Mary E. 1979. Principles of Women's Intercollegiate
     Athletics. Ph.D. diss., University of Southern California.

Lexikon Der 14000 Olympioniken: Who's Who at the Olympics.
     1983. Graz, Austria: Leykam.

Libman, Gary. 1977. Lynne Cox. Mankato, Minn.: Cre-
     ative Education.

McGinnis, Vera. 1974. Rodeo Road: My Life as a Pioneer
     Cowgirl. New York: Hastings House.

Macksey, Joan, and Kenneth M. Macksey. 1975. The Book
     of Women's Achievements. New York: Stein & Day.

McWhirter, Norris, Steve Morgenstern, Roz Morgenstern, and
     Stan Greenberg. 1979. Guinness Book of Women's Sports
     Records. New York: Sterling.

Markel, Robert, and Nancy Brooks. 1985. For the Record:
     Women in Sports. New York: Ballantine Books.

Marin, Nea. 1968. A Woman's Reach: Mountaineering Mem-
     oirs. New York: Dodd, Mead.

Martin, Ann. 1979. The Equestrian Woman. New York:
     Grosset & Dunlap.

_____. 1976. Martina Navratilova: Tennis Fury. St.
     Paul: EMC.

_____. 1975. Mary Decker: Speed Records and Spaghetti.
     St. Paul: EMC.

May, Julian. 1975. Janet Lynn: Figure Skating Star.
     Mankato, Minn.: Crestwood House.

_____. 1974. Billie Jean King: Tennis Champion.
Mankato, Minn.: Crestwood House.

Meade, Marion. 1975. Women in Sports: Tennis. New
York: Harvey House.

Miklowitz, Gloria D. 1978. Tracy Austin. New York:
Grosset & Dunlap.

Morse, Ann. 1976. Tennis Champion, Billie Jean King.
Mankato, Minn.: Creative Education.

_____. 1975. Janet Lynn. Mankato, Minn.: Creative
Education.

Morse, Charles, and Ann Morse. 1974. Peggy Fleming.
Mankato, Minn.: Creative Education.

The National Sports Review. 1987. Seattle: Preview Publishing and Infosports [sports records set in 1987].

Nickerson, Elinor. 1987. Golf: A Women's History.
Jefferson, N.C.: McFarland.

Nyad, Diana. 1978. Other Shores. New York: Random
House [long-distance swimming].

Olsen, James T. 1976. One Hundred Greatest Women in
Sports. New York: Grosset & Dunlap.

_____. 1974. Billie Jean King: The Lady of the Court.
Mankato, Minn.: Creative Education.

O'Shea, Mary Jo. 1977. Winning Tennis Star: Chris Evert.
Mankato, Minn.: Creative Education.

_____. 1976. Laura Baugh. Mankato, Minn.: Creative
Education.

Phillips, Betty Lou. 1977. Chris Evert, First Lady of
Tennis. New York: Julian Messner.

Reichler, Joseph L. 1983. The Macmillan Baseball Calendar:
1984. New York: Macmillan.

Remley, Mary L.   1980.   Women in Sport: A Guide to Infor-
     mation Sources.   Detroit: Gale Research.

Robertson, Max, ed.   1976.   Robin Campbell: Joy in the
     Morning.   St. Paul: EMC.

_____.   1974.   The Encyclopedia of Tennis.   New York:
     Viking.

Robison, Nancy.   1978.   Tracy Austin, Teenage Superstar.
     New York: Harvey House.

_____.   1975.   Rosemary Casals: The Rebel Rosebud.
     St. Paul: EMC.

Russell, Alan, and Norris McWhirter, eds.   1987.   1988
     Guinness Book of World Records.   New York: Sterling.

Ryan, Joan.   1975.   Contributions of Women: Sports.
     Minneapolis: Dillon Press.

Sabin, Francene.   1977.   Set Point: The Story of Chris
     Evert.   New York: G. P. Putnam's Sons.

_____.   1975.   Women Who Win.   New York: Random
     House.

Schmitz, Dorothy C.   1977.   Dorothy Hamill: Skate to Vic-
     tory.   Mankato, Minn.:   Crestwood House.

Schoor, Gene.   1978.   Babe Didrikson: The World's Great-
     est Woman Athlete.   Garden City, N.Y.:   Doubleday.

Scott, Eugene.   1973.   Tennis: A Game of Motion.   New
     York: Crown Publishers.

Shane, George.   1975.   Sportraits of the Stars.   Toronto:
     Gall Publications.

Smith, Beatrice S.   1976.   Babe: Mildred Didrikson Zaharias.
     Milwaukee: Raintree Publications.

Smith, Hay H.   1975.   Chris Evert.   Mankato, Minn.:
     Creative Education.

Smith, Kibbe. 1983. Sports Calendar for 1984. New York: Workman Publishing.

Smith, Miranda G. 1977. Dorothy Hamill. Mankato, Minn.: Creative Education.

Soucheray, Joe. 1977. Sheila Young. Mankato, Minn.: Creative Education.

Spears, Betty, ed. 1974. "The Emergence of Women in Sport." In Barbara Hoepner, ed. Women's Athletics: Coping with Controversy. Washington: AAHPER.

_____, and Richard A. Swanson. 1983. History of Sport and Physical Activity in the United States. Dubuque: William C. Brown.

Stambler, Irwin. 1973. Speed Kings: World's Fastest Humans. New York: Doubleday.

_____. 1975. Women in Sports. Garden City, N.Y.: Doubleday.

Sterling, Robert M., and Mark Looy. 1986. Athletes Tell Their Unforgettable Moments in Sport. Champaign, Ill.: Leisure Press.

Sullivan, George. 1974. Queens of the Court. New York: Dodd, Mead.

Thacher, Alida M. 1976. Raising a Racket: Rosemary Casals. Milwaukee: Raintree Editions.

Underhill, Miriam. 1971. Give Me the Hills. Riverside, Conn.: Chatham Press.

U.S. Congress. 92nd Congress (June 1972). Public Law 92-318: The Education Amendments of 1972.

Van Steenwyk, Elizabeth. 1978. Peggy Fleming: Cameo of a Champion. New York: McGraw-Hill.

_____. 1976. Women in Sports: Figure Skating. New York: Harvey House.

_____. 1978. Women in Sports: Rodeo. New York:
    Harvey House.

Wade, Paul. 1983. Winning Women: The Changing Image of
    Women in Sports. New York: Times Books.

Walter, Claire. 1977. Women in Sports: Skiing. New
    York: Harvey House.

Williams, Cicely. 1975. Wilma Rudolph: Run for Glory.
    St. Paul: EMC.

_____. 1975. Wimbledon World Tennis Focus. Mankato,
    Minn.: Creative Education.

_____. 1973. Women on the Rope. London: George
    Allen & Unwin [mountaineering].

The World Almanac and Book of Facts. 1987. New York:
    World Almanac.

Periodicals

Long Beach Press-Telegram
Los Angeles Times
New York Times
New York Times Index
Orange County Register
Runner's World
San Diego Union
Smith Alumnae Quarterly
USA Today
Women's Sports and Fitness

ORGANIZATIONS

We thank the following organizations for sharing their information and their time:

Amateur Athletic Union of the United States. 3400 West 86th Street, Indianapolis, Ind. 46268

Amateur Fencers' League of America. 601 Curtis Street, Albany, Calif. 94706

Amateur Softball Association of America. 2801 Northeast 50th Street, Oklahoma City, Okla. 73112

Amateur Trapshooting Association. P.O. Box 246, West National Road, Vandalia, Ohio 45399

Amateur Trapshooting Association Hall of Fame. Vandalia, Ohio 45377

American Athletic Association for the Deaf. 3916 Lantern Avenue, Silver Spring, Md. 20902

American Bicycle Hall of Fame. 260 West 260th Street, New York, N.Y. 10471

American Canoe Association. P.O. Box 248, Lorton, Va. 22079

American Casting Association. Picnic Hill, Jackson, Ky. 41339

American Junior Bowling Congress. 5301 South 76th Street, Greendale, Wis. 53129

American Motorcyclist Association. P.O. Box 141, Westerville, Ohio 43081

American Platform Tennis Association. Box 901, Upper Mont-
clair, N.J. 07043

American Rowing Association. 824 Amies Lane, Bryn Mawr,
Pa. 19010

American Water Ski Association. 799 Overlook Drive, Winter
Haven, Fla. 33882

Appalachian Mountain Club. 5 Joy Street, Boston, Mass.
02108

Arizona Women's Bowling Association Hall of Fame. Box
11435, Phoenix, Ariz. 85061

Center for Women and Sport. White Building, Pennsylvania
State University, University Park, Pa. 16802

Citizens Savings Athletic Foundation (formerly Helms Athletic
Foundation). 9800 South Sepulveda Boulevard, Los
Angeles, Calif. 90045

Eastern Association of Rowing Colleges. P.O. Box 3, Centerville, Mass. 02632

Eastern Tennis Patrons. 22 East 49th Street, New York,
N.Y. 10017

Feminist Karate Union. Suite 250A, 101 Nickerson, Seattle,
Wash. 98109

Girls Rodeo Association. 8909 Northeast 25th Street, Spencer,
Okla. 73084

Intercollegiate Rowing Association. P.O. Box 3, Centerville,
Mass. 02632

Inter-Collegiate Yacht Racing Association of North America.
8893 Melinda Court, Milan, Mich. 48160

International Amateur Swimming Federation. 2000 Financial
Center, Des Moines, Iowa 50309

International Side-Saddle Organization. R.D. 2, Box 2096,
Mount Holly, N.J. 08060

International Swimming Hall of Fame.   One Hall of Fame Drive,
   Fort Lauderdale, Fla. 33316

International Tennis Hall of Fame.   194 Bellevue Avenue,
   Newport, R.I. 02840

International Women's Fishing Association.   P.O. Box 2025,
   Palm Beach, Fla. 33480

Iowa Women's Bowling Association Hall of Fame.   1615 Pierce,
   Sioux City, Iowa 51105

Ladies Professional Golf Hall of Fame.   Augusta Golf and
   Country Club, Augusta, Ga. 30903

League of American Wheelmen.   P.O. Box 988, Baltimore,
   Md. 21203

Los Angeles Aiki Kai (Aikido).   8929 Ellis Avenue, Los
   Angeles, Calif. 90034

Mesa Valley Women's Bowling Association Hall of Fame.   1833
   East Nielsen, Mesa, Ariz. 85204

Middle States Regatta Association.   C/o Fairmount Rowing
   Association, 2 Boathouse Row, Philadelphia, Pa. 19130

Motormaids.   556 West 4th Street, Chillicothe, Ohio 45601

Naismith Memorial Basketball Hall of Fame.   Box 175, Alden
   Street, Highland Station, Springfield, Mass. 01109

National Archery Association of the United States.   1951
   Geraldson Drive, Lancaster, Pa. 17601

National Cowboy Hall of Fame and Heritage Center.   1700 NE
   63rd Street, Oklahoma City, Okla. 73111

National Duckpin Bowling Congress.   711 14th Street NW,
   Washington, D.C.   20005

National Federation of State High School Associations.
   11724 Plaza Circle, P.O. Box 20626, Kansas City, Mo.
   64195

National Field Archery Association. Route 2, Box 514, Red-
lands, Calif. 92373

National Horseshoe Pitchers Association of America. P.O.
Box 1702, Auburn, Calif. 95603

National Intercollegiate Women's Fencing Association. 18
Pleasant Place, Kearny, N.J. 07032

National Junior College Athletic Association. P.O. Box 1586,
Hutchinson, Kans. 67501

National Muzzle Loading Rifle Association. Friendship, Ind.
47021

National Rifle Association of America. 1600 Rhode Island
Avenue NW, Washington, D.C. 20036

National Rowing Foundation. P.O. Box 6030, Arlington, Va.
22206

National Skeet Shooting Association. P.O. Box 28188, San
Antonio, Tex. 78228

National Ski Hall of Fame. National Headquarters Division,
P.O. Box 191, Ishpeming, Mich. 49849

National Softball Hall of Fame. 2801 Northeast 50th Street,
Oklahoma City, Okla. 73112

National Track and Field Hall of Fame. 1524 Kanawha Boulevard East, Charleston, W.Va. 25311

NOW Task Force on Women in Sports. National NOW Action
Center, Suite 1001, 425 13th Street NW, Washington, D.C.
20004

Professional Archers Association. 4711 South Brennan
Road, Hemlock, Mich. 48626

Road Runners Club of America. 1226 Orchard Village,
Manchester, Mo. 63011

San Diego Hall of Champions. 1439 El Prado, Balboa Park,
San Diego, Calif. 92101

Soaring Society of America. Box 66071, Los Angeles, Calif.
  90066

Special Olympics. Suite 203, 1701 K Street NW, Washington,
  D.C. 20006

Texas Women's Bowling Association Hall of Fame. 117 Melbourne, Fort Worth, Tex. 76117

Track and Field Association of the United States of America.
  10920 Ambassador Drive, Kansas City, Mo. 64153

Underwater Society of America. 732 50th Street, West Palm
  Beach, Fla. 33407

United States Badminton Association. P.O. Box 237, Swartz
  Creek, Mich. 48473

United States Duffers Association. P.O. Box 283, Newport,
  Ky. 41072

United States Golf Association. Golf House, Far Hills, N.J.
  07931

United States Handball Federation. 4101 Dempster Street,
  Skokie, Ill. 60076

United States Judo Federation. 21054 Sarah Hills Drive,
  Saratoga, Calif. 95070

United States Parachute Association. Suite 444, 806 15th
  Street NW, Washington, D.C. 20005

United States Polo Association. Executive Plaza, Suite 706,
  Oak Brook, Ill. 60521

United States Racquetball Association. 4101 Dempster Street,
  Skokie, Ill. 60076

United States Revolver Association. 59 Alvin Street, Springfield, Mass. 01104

United States Rowing Association. Suite 980, 251 North
  Illinois Street, Indianapolis, Ind. 46204

United States Rowing Society. Suite 980, 251 North Illinois
Street, Indianapolis, Ind. 46204

United States Table Tennis Association. 1031 Jackson Street,
St. Charles, Mo. 63301

United States Tennis Association. 51 East 42nd Street, New
York, N.Y. 10017

United States Volleyball Association. 1750 East Boulder,
Colorado Springs, Colo. 80909

United States Women's Curling Association. 1201 Somerset
Drive, Glenview, Ill. 60025

United States Women's Lacrosse Association. R.D. 2, Boiling
Springs, Pa. 17001

United States Yacht Racing Union. P.O. Box 209, Newport,
R.I. 02840

Women's Equity Action League. 805 15th Street NW, Washington, D.C. 20005

Women's International Bowling Congress. 5301 South 76th
Street, Greendale, Wis. 53129

Women's International Bowling Congress Hall of Fame. 5301
South 76th Street, Greendale, Wis. 53129

Women's Professional Billiard Alliance Hall of Fame. 17 Strong
Place, Brooklyn, N.Y. 11231

Women's Sports Foundation. Suite 728, 342 Madison Avenue,
New York, N.Y. 10173

Women's Tennis Association. 1604 Union Street, San Francisco, Calif. 94123

World Golf Hall of Fame. P.O. Box 908, Pinehurst, N.C.
28374

INDEX OF NAMES

Metzger, Debra 89, 93
Meyer, Debbie 50, 52, 55
Meyers, Ann 75, 84
Michal, Donna 91
Mikiel, Val 22, 23, 25, 84
Miller, Cheryl 98, 101, 104
Miller, Dorothy 30, 41
Miller, Kim 79
Miller, Michele 111
Minions, Kaye 74
Mitchell, Betsy 105
Mitchell, Donna 95
Mitchell, Linda 27
Mitchell, Michele 105
Mitchell, Virne "Jackie" 14
Moe, Karen 61
Moffitt, Billie Jean see King,
    Billie Jean
Molburg, Deborah 77
Molitor, Wendy 99
Monez, Karen E. 105, 112
Moody, Helen Wills 8, 9, 10,
    16
Moon, April 77
Moore, Sherryl 81, 94
Moran, Gertrude "Gussie"
    24
Morgan, Dottie 70
Morreau, Janet 28
Morris, Betty 75
Morris, Pam 47
Mraz, Jo 37
Mudge, Genevra 2
Muldowney, Shirley "Cha Cha"
    79
Murdock, Margaret 57, 73
Murphy, Paula 46, 76
Myers, Cheryl 116
Myers, Joyce A. 105
Myler, Cammy 110
Myrick, Nancy 47, 50, 57

Natrass, Susan 68, 77
Navratilova, Martina 80, 83,
    86, 89, 93, 97, 100, 103,
    106, 112
Neer, Phil 16
Nelson, Frankie 2
Nelson, Vicky 100
Netter, Mildrette 53
Newkirk, Florence Chambers
    9, 58
Neyer, Megan 105, 111
Nichols, Lorie 60
Nicholson, Nellie 75, 83
Nielson, Sandy 59, 61
Norelius, Martha 8, 11, 12,
    50
Notaro, Phyllis 28, 84
Notorangelo, Susan 104
Nyad, Diana 82

Oakley, Annie 1, 7
Oberg, Margo Godfrey 55
Ochs, Debra J. 93, 97
Olson, Zoe Ann 23
O'Neill, Kitty 76
O'Rourke, Heidi 55, 57, 59,
    62
Ortner, Beverly 54, 56, 63
Osipowich, Albina 11
Outerbridge, Mary Ewing
    xiv
Overton, Kristi 109

Palzo, Cathey 109
Parker, Denise 111
Parmentier, Gloria K. 105
Pasquale, Claudia 89
Peeney, Betsy 45
Pelletier, Debi 99
Pelosi, Carol 72
Pennington, Mary-Jean 80
Peppler, Mary Jo 51, 54,
    71
Perrin, Ethel 2
Phaler, Emma 10, 48
Phelan, Jacquie 99, 102,
    104
Phillips, Joyce 107

INDEX OF SPORTS